I0182694

BIBLE TEACHINGS
A Summary View of Christian Doctrine Drawn from the Word of God

By Joseph Stump

BIBLE TEACHINGS
BY JOSEPH STUMP

Just & Sinner
1467 Walnut Ave.
Brighton, IA 52540

www.JustandSinner.com

ISBN 10: 0692216820
ISBN 13: 978-0692216828

TABLE OF CONTENTS

CHAPTER I. CONCERNING GOD. THAT GOD IS. WHO AND WHAT HE IS.

It is only through the Bible that we can learn to know God.

Conscience.—It is true, men know even without the Bible that there is a Higher Being. The belief in the existence of God is implanted in every heart, and is found among all nations, even the most barbarous and degraded (Rom. 1:19). All men have a conscience which teaches them to distinguish between good and evil, and bids them expect punishment from a divine judge if they do wrong.

The Order of the World.—The works of nature confirm this natural belief in the existence of God. "The heavens declare the glory of God. The expanse shows his handiwork" (Psalm 19:1). The very fact that the world exists demands that there be One who has created it. And in the variety, order and beauty apparent in nature on every hand, in the alternation of day and night, in the succession of the seasons, and in the marvelous manner in which the earth is adapted to supply the wants of the creatures who dwell upon it, there is so evident a proof of wise and beneficial design, that none but a fool can say, "All this came into existence by itself or by chance."

The Bible Needed.—But neither conscience nor nature can give a sufficient and saving knowledge of God. Left to this natural knowledge, men became idolaters, and "traded the glory of the incorruptible God for the likeness of an image of corruptible man, and of birds, and four-footed animals, and creeping things" (Rom. 1:23). It is not sufficient to know that there is a God. We must know what kind of a God He is, how we can be received into His love, and how we should live in His sight. This we can learn only from the Bible. Let us see, therefore, what the Bible teaches about God.

The Three in One.—There is but one God. When He gave His commandments to men, God said, "I am the Lord your God; you shall have no other gods before Me" (Exod. 20:3). But, although there is only one God, there are three Persons, Father, Son and Holy Ghost. Hence we speak of God as the Trinity, or the Three in One. Of these three Persons, none is greater or less than the other, but all are equal in every respect. "The Father is God, the Son is God, and the Holy Ghost is God. And yet there are not three Gods but one God" (Athanasian Creed). This is a mystery that we cannot comprehend. It is not to be expected that we should. The finite cannot comprehend the infinite. There are many things in the world around us which we cannot understand. How can we understand Him who created the world? What we can and are to do is to receive the knowledge of God as He Himself has revealed it to us.

The three Persons of the Holy Trinity are named in Christ's command to His disciples, when He said, "Go therefore and make disciples of all nations, baptizing them in the name of the Father and of the Son and of the Holy Spirit" (Matt. 28:19). And they are revealed at Christ's baptism, where the Holy Ghost descended on Christ in the form of a dove, and the Father spoke from heaven and said, "This is my beloved Son, with whom I am well pleased" (Matt. 3:17).

What God Is.—God is a Spirit. He therefore has no body and no limbs and senses as we have. We sometimes speak of God's almighty arm and His all-seeing eye. The Scriptures themselves sometimes speak of Him in this manner. But this way of speaking is used simply to accommodate our idea of God to human ways of thinking, because for us power to do lies in the arm, and power to see in the eye. God is a Spirit of infinite power and majesty, without limits or bounds, and of absolute perfection. "He fills heaven and earth" (Jer. 23:24).

He is Eternal. There never was a time when God was not, and there never will be a time when He is not. He is from everlasting to everlasting. He is Unchangeable. He Himself declares, "I the Lord do not change" (Mal. 3:6). He is the same yesterday, today and forever. What He now is He always has been and always will be. He is Omnipresent, that is, He is present everywhere at the same time. There is no nook or corner of the wide universe where God is not. He is ever beside us, wherever we may be. He is Omniscient, that is, He knows all things. Past, present and future are equally present to His view. Nothing can escape His knowledge. He reads and knows every thought, desire and purpose of our hearts. He is Omnipotent or Almighty. His power is unlimited. Nothing is impossible with God, though of course He cannot do anything which is in conflict with His own nature, such as to lie or do evil of any kind.

In His Relation to us.—1. **God is Holy**. The angels who stand before His throne continually sing, "Holy, Holy, Holy is the Lord God of Hosts. The whole earth is full of His glory" (Is. 6:3). He is holy Himself and demands that we be holy also. 2. **He is Just**. He requires the fulfilment of His holy laws, and will punish the guilty, rendering to every man according to his deeds. 3. **He is All-wise**. He always knows what is best to be done, and what is the best way to accomplish His ends. 4. **He is Kind and Merciful, He is Love itself**. He is kind even to the unthankful; for, "He makes His sun to rise on the evil and on the good, and sends rain on the righteous and on the wicked" (Matt. 5:54). His mercies are new unto us every morning. He has "no pleasure in the death of the wicked, but that the wicked turn from His way and live" (Ez. 33:11). His love to the world is so great that "He gave His only-begotten Son that whosoever believes on Him should not perish, but have everlasting life" (John 3:16). He bears long with the impenitent and desires to lead them to repentance by His goodness. 5. **He is Faithful and True.** He will do all that He has threatened or promised. He is the one Being in all the universe on whom absolute reliance may be placed.

CHAPTER II. GOD MADE, MAINTAINS, AND RULES THE WORLD.

God Made the World.—The world did not always exist, nor did it come into being by itself or by chance. It is the work of God. He alone is from eternity: all other things had a beginning and have their source and origin in Him; for "of Him and through Him and to Him are all things" (Rom. 11:36). He willed that the world should be, and it came into being. "He spoke and it was done." He commanded and it stood fast" (Ps. 33:9).

The Manner in which God made the world is described in the first two chapters of the Bible. "In the beginning God created the heaven and the earth."(Gen. 1:1). He made them out of nothing. The heaven and earth thus created were not, however, the beautiful heaven and earth we now behold, but a formless, shapeless mass,—the raw material out of which God subsequently in six days fashioned the world as it now is. At first "the earth was without form and void, and darkness was upon the face of the deep" (Gen. 1:2). But "the Spirit of God moved upon the face of the waters," (Gen. 1:2) preparing the shapeless, lifeless mass for the creative Word. And then in six successive "days" God (1) created the light and separated it from the darkness, (2) made the firmament, (3) divided the dry land from the sea and covered it with plant life, (4) set the sun, moon and stars in their places, (5) made the fishes and the birds, (6) the beasts of the field and finally man. On the seventh day God rested from His work, and hallowed the day.

The Creation of Man was the last and crowning work. For, "God created man in His own image, in the image of God created He him; male and female created He them" (Gen. 1:27). He "formed man of the dust of the ground, and breathed into his nostrils the breath of life; and man became a living soul" (Gen. 2:7). Woman was made to be a helpmate for man, and was created by God out of a rib taken from man's side while he was asleep. Creation is the work of the Triune God. The Son and the Holy Ghost took part in it with the Father. But it is ascribed to God the Father by pre-eminence. It is thus ascribed to Him in the Apostles' Creed.

God Maintains the World.—God did not create the world and then let it exist by itself, nor let it run like a watch or clock till it is worn out. He constantly maintains and preserves what He Las made. If He did not, the world would at once fall into ruin. For what the apostle says of men is true of all created things: "In Him we live and move and have our being" (Acts 17:28). He who made "the heaven and the earth and all things that are therein, serves them all" (Neh. 9:6). His tender mercies are over all His works, from the largest of the fixed stars of the universe down to the birds of the air and the grass of the field.

God's Care for Man.—While God preserves and watches over all His works, He exercises special Providential, care over man. He is not far from every one of us. When God created man He promised to supply his wants. And He has done so ever since that time. The farmer sows the grain, but God makes it grow. The eyes of all wait upon Him, and He gives them their meat in due season. It is He who opens His liberal hand and satisfies the desires of every living thing.

God's Particular Care for the Godly.—The care which God exercises over men in general, He bestows in special measure upon the godly. "The eye of the Lord is upon them that fear Him; upon them that hope in His mercy: to deliver their soul from death, and to keep them alive in famine" (Ps. 33:18-19). Believers are told, therefore, to cast all their care upon Him, because He cares for them (1 Pet. 5:7). He who feeds the fowls of the air and clothes the lilies of the field will much more feed and clothe His children (Matt. 6:27). He, without whose knowledge not even a sparrow falls, watches much more closely over the believers, because they are of more value than many sparrows (Matt. 10:29). So full and minute is His care and forethought for them, that even the very hairs upon their head are all numbered.

God Rules the World.—God reigns supreme over the universe which He has made. He is Lord over all, the blessed and only Potentate, the King of kings and the Lord of lords. He rules over nations and individuals. While there are many things in His government which are not clear to us in this world, and His thoughts are not our thoughts nor our ways His ways, He sees to it that "all things shall work together for good to them that love Him" (Rom. 8:28). He permits many things to happen which He does not desire. Thus He permits men to sin, if they will, because they are responsible moral beings and not mere machines. But beyond the limits which He lays down no creature can go. He often, for His own wise purposes, permits the wicked to prosper and the godly to suffer. But He sets bounds to the suffering of His children, and permits only so much to come upon them as will conduce to their final good.

God blesses the undertakings of the godly. On the other hand He frequently hinders the purposes of evil men. He prevented Laban from injuring Jacob, and Balaam from cursing Israel. And He frequently overrules men's action so as to bring good out of evil.

Thus he made the selling of Joseph into slavery by his brethren the means of saving Jacob's family as well as the whole population of Egypt from death by famine, and the crucifixion of Jesus by the wicked Jews the means of redeeming the human race from destruction.

CHAPTER III. HOW GOD MADE MAN IN HIS OWN IMAGE. HOW MAN FELL INTO SIN AND BECAME A LOST BEING.

Man Made in God's Image.—Man, who was the last, is also the highest and noblest of God's earthly creatures. He is so, because he "is made after the likeness of God" (James 3:9), and "is the image and glory of God" (1 Cor. 11:7). For when God had done everything necessary to make the earth a fit and pleasant abode for man, and had made the inferior creatures, He said, "Let us make man in our image, after our likeness" (Gen. 1:26). It is this image or likeness of God which places man so far above the brute, and which makes the slaying of a human being a crime that is to be punished with death.

Man's Body.—This image or likeness of God in which man was created was not a bodily one; for God is a Spirit and has no body. On the physical side of his being, man is akin to the beasts. His body like theirs was made of the dust of the ground. Though it is a most marvelous piece of divine workmanship and is vastly superior to the bodies of the lower animals, it is only the tabernacle in which the soul dwells. Yet the body also possesses a dignity of its own; for it is the handiwork of God, it was assumed by the Son of God when lie became man, and, in the case of the believer, it is the temple of the Holy Ghost in this world and shall be transformed and glorified in the world to come.

Man's Soul—Man's real self is his soul or spirit, which God breathed into him at creation. It is this soul that was made in the image of God and was a likeness or reflection of Him. Man, being a creature, could not, of course, be made like God in all things. Only the Son of God Jesus Christ, is the image of God in this full and complete sense. He is "the brightness of God's glory and the express image of His person" (Heb. 9:3). But man was created in the image and after the likeness of God; that is, God gave to man in a limited and finite measure those faculties and powers which He Himself possesses in unlimited and infinite measure. For God created man with reason and understanding, with a free will, with power to do what was good, with immortality, with dominion over the other creatures, and especially with a clear knowledge of God, perfect righteousness and true holiness. In his original state man was a perfect being, who enjoyed God's favor and blessing, and who was perfectly happy.

Man's Fall Into Sin.—Man was placed by God in the garden of Eden to dress and keep it, and was given permission to eat of every tree in the garden except the tree of the knowledge of good and evil. Of this tree he was forbidden to eat on pain of death. His obedience to God was now put to the test. He was not to do God's will by compulsion, but voluntarily. He was created with a free will and was now to choose between obedience and disobedience. Had he chosen to obey, all would have been well. But the devil, who is the source of all evil, came to Eve under the guise of a serpent and deceived her. He persuaded her to doubt God's threat of punishment, filled her soul with a longing to taste of the forbidden fruit, and prevailed on her to eat of it. Eve then gave some of the fruit to her husband; and Adam, though not deceived as she had been, listened to the persuasions of his wife and ate also.

The Consequences of the Fall.—By this sin man fell from his state of purity and happiness, was expelled from Eden, brought upon himself bodily and spiritual death, and became a lost being. And since all men are descended from Adam, they all inherit from him the consequences of the Fall.

Bodily Death.—God had said to Adam, "In the day that you eat of it, you will surely die" (Gen. 2:17). And although Adam was permitted to reach the age of 930 years before he died, he became a dying creature from the moment when he disobeyed the command of God. Man's body is now a mortal body, and shall return to the earth from where it came. It is appointed unto men once to die, though they know not when nor where, because they know not what shall be on the morrow. Their life is frail as a flower and fleeting as a shadow. If it is a long life, it reaches seventy or eighty years, and at its best it is full of labor and sorrow. The whole human race has inherited the curse which God pronounced upon Adam and Eve immediately after their transgression, together with all the ills, pain and disease that are inseparable from a mortal body.

Spiritual Death.—But the most direful effects of the Fall are felt in man's soul. He still has, indeed, reason and understanding; but they are by no means as strong as they were before the Fall. He still possesses dominion over the inferior creatures; but it is very much limited. He still has a free will in earthly matters and can decide for himself what he will do in things that concern this world; but he has lost his free will in spiritual matters and can no longer by his own power do anything but that which is evil. The imagination of his heart is evil from his youth. He has lost the knowledge of God and the righteousness and holiness which he originally possessed. And now all men are born with a sinful nature and an inherited inclination to evil. This corruptness of our nature is called original sin. It leads to actual sins as soon as men are old enough to act. It grows into evil deeds as naturally and inevitably as the acorn grows into the oak. Separated by the Fall from God who is the source of all life, man is spiritually dead and doomed to eternal destruction, until he is born again by the grace of God and is renewed after the image of God in righteousness and true holiness. And even then the old sinful nature remains as a law in the flesh that wars against the law of the spirit,—a law which must be fought against and overcome more and more in this world, but which will never completely disappear till we are transformed and glorified in the world to come.

CHAPTER IV. THE JUSTICE OF GOD MUST DEMAND MAN'S CONDEMNATION.

God's Will is the Law for all His creatures; for He is King and Lord over all. Human life and development according to God's will would have meant perfection and unbroken happiness to the race.

How God Gave Men His Law.—God wrote His law in man's heart at creation as part of the image of God. But this original knowledge of God's will became more and more obscured after the Fall into sin. Therefore at Mt. Sinai God gave men His law anew, written on two tables of stone. This law is known as the Moral Law or the Ten Commandments. It is also called the Decalogue. The sum and substance of this law, as Christ Himself tells us, is: "You shall love the Lord thy God with all your heart, and with all your soul, and with all your mind," and "You shall love your neighbor as yourself" (Matt. 22:37).

How He Threatens Transgressors.—God requires men to keep His law on pain of punishment. When He gave men the Ten Commandments. He said, "I the Lord your God am a jealous God, visiting the iniquities of the fathers upon the children to the third and fourth generation of them that hate Me" (Ex. 20:5). And elsewhere in the Bible He says, "Cursed is every one that continues not in all the things that are written in the book of the law to do them" (Gal. 3:10), "the wages of sin is death" (Rom. 6:23), and "the soul that sins shall die" (Ez. 18:4).

Man Has Broken God's Law.—Man is sinful and guilty in God's sight. He is a sinful being by birth; for he is born of sinful parents, and "that which is born of the flesh is flesh" (John 3:6). He is by nature a child of wrath. His mind is enmity against God, and is not subject to God's law. His heart is a hard, stony, and rebellious heart, lacking the fear and love of God, and filled with the love of self and the world. It is deceitful above all things and desperately wicked. It is a foul fountain of sin and iniquity.

He sins against God daily by thought, word and deed. He does many things which God has forbidden, and omits many things which God has commanded. His transgressions are innumerable. He often does wrong without even knowing it. Therefore the Psalmist prays, "Cleanse me from secret faults" (Ps. 19:12). As long as the fear and love of God are absent from man's heart, everything that he does is sinful, because he does not act from the right motive. The only kind of actions that are pleasing to God are those that are done out of love to Him; for "love is the fulfilling of the law" (Rom. 13:16).

All Men are Guilty.—There is no difference between men with respect to God's law. "All have sinned and come short of the glory of God" (Rom. 3:23). "There is not a just man upon earth that does good and does not sin" (Eccl. 7:20). The only sinless Being who ever trod the earth since the Fall into sin is Jesus Christ our Lord. He "did no sin, neither was guile found in his mouth" (1 Pet. 2:22). All others are sinful in heart and life. "They are all gone out of the way," and "there is none that doeth good, no not one." Some have gone out of the way farther than others, and have committed more flagrant sins. But "there is none righteous, no not one" (Rom. 3:12). The best man, as well as the worst, is a breaker of God's law and guilty in His sight.[1] The Pharisee, who thought himself holy and thanked God that he was not as other men are, was a sinner as well as the publican who stood near him. The Jews, who boasted that they were the children of Abraham and had the law, were sinners as well as the Gentiles whom they despised. And "if we say we have no sin, we deceive ourselves, and the truth is not in us" (1 John 1:8).

All Deserve Punishment.—Being transgressors of God's law, men deserve to be punished. Punishment is the just and necessary outcome of sin. Earthly governments do and must punish offenders, if they would not be unjust to those citizens who keep the laws. Who would want to live under a government that permits the thief and the murderer to go unpunished? Just so the justice of God, who governs the universe, requires the punishment of men, because they have broken His laws. If He did not inflict that punishment, He would not only break His own word which says that He will punish, but also be unfair and unjust to those of His creatures who, like the good angels, keep all His laws. To make light of sin is, therefore, the part of a

---

[1] The prevalence of crime, drunkenness, Impurity and divorce; the eager desire to get rich, the unlawful power of money, the corruption of politics, the selfishness and utter lack of consideration for others so often manifested in business life, the crushing of the individual on the stock exchange, the cruelty of competition; slyness, deceit, pride, inordinate self-esteem, revengefulness, malice, hatred and envy in people who are usually regarded as comparatively good;—all this, and much more which might be mentioned, illustrates the truthfulness of the Bible's description of the depravity of the natural heart and life.

fool. Sin inevitably exposes men to the everlasting wrath of God. It will not be overlooked or excused by Him. "For the Lord is righteous" (Ps. 129:4), "justice and judgment are the habitation of His throne" (Ps. 89:13).

God Will Punish.—Men may deceive themselves as to the consequences of their sins. But "God is not mocked" (Gal. 6:7). His wrath will certainly come upon the children of disobedience may be delayed, but it will come at last.

In This World.—God frequently punishes men in this world. He punishes them through the pains and sufferings which, though delayed, sooner or later come as a retribution upon those who break the laws of nature and of nature's God. Men cannot sin with impunity. Drunkards and licentious persons bring misery upon themselves and upon others, and shorten their own life by their sins. Children often are made to suffer in body, mind and property on account of the sins of their parents.

God punishes the criminals through the penalties which earthly governments inflict for crimes; for earthly governments are His ministers "to execute wrath upon him does evil" (Rom. 13:4). And He often sends punishment in the form of special judgments, such as accidents, sickness, or reverses of one kind or another. Famine, pestilence, conflagrations and the like are frequently a punishment which God sends upon whole communities for their sins. The flood, the destruction of Sodom and Gomorrah and of the Canaanite nations, the downfall of Nineveh and Babylon and other ancient nations were a judgment of God upon sin. The fall of the Roman empire may be directly traced to its corruption and wickedness.[2]

---

[2] We dare not, however, conclude when pain or suffering is brought upon anyone, that he is being punished. God also brings suffering upon the good for

In the Next World.—Unless men repent and are forgiven for Christ's sake, God will punish them eternally in the world to come. They who continue in their sins and harden their hearts are "treasuring up for themselves wrath against the day of wrath and revelation of the righteous vengeance of God" (Rom. 2:5). For there will come a time when God will "render to every man according to his deeds" (Rom. 2:6), a day of reckoning, when the wicked shall cry out in despair to the mountains, "Fall on us and hide us from the face of Him that sits on the throne and from the wrath of the Lamb; for the great day of His wrath is come, and who shall be able to stand?" (Rev. 6:16-17). Then shall the wicked be cast out into utter darkness, there shall be weeping and gnashing of teeth. They shall have their part with the devil and his angels in the lake that burns with fire; and the smoke of their torment shall ascend forever and ever.

---

purposes of chastening. Whom the Lord loveth, He chasteneth."—Heb. 12:6.

CHAPTER V. THE LOVE OF GOD HAS PREPARED A WAY FOR MAN'S SALVATION.

A judge dare not relax the law or refuse to pass sentence upon a criminal because that criminal happens to be his son. If he did, he would be an unjust judge and unfit for the position which he occupies. But while as a judge he necessarily pronounces condemnation upon his son, as a father his heart is filled with love, and he spares no efforts to help, rescue and save his boy from the sin and error of his way. It is so with God. As Law-giver and Judge He is obliged to pass the sentence of condemnation on man. But as our Father, whose heart is filled with love to us, He desires our salvation. And therefore we find that, while on the one hand God's justice demands man's punishment, on the other hand His love has prepared a way by which all men may be saved, if they will.

God Loves Man.—God reveals His love to us in the earthly blessings which He bestows upon us. We deserve none at His hands, yet He daily showers His benefits upon us. For "every good gift and every perfect gift" which we enjoy in this world "is from above, and cometh down from the Father of lights with whom there is no variableness neither shadow of turning" (James 1:17). "The earth is full of the goodness of the Lord" (Ps. 33:5).

But God reveals His love especially in what He has done and is willing to do for man's soul. "For God so loved the world that He gave His only begotten Son, that whosoever believes on Him should not perish, but have everlasting life" (John 3:16). And "eye hath not seen nor ear heard, neither have entered into the heart of man the things which God has prepared for them that love Him" (1 Cor. 2:9).

God Loved Man From all Eternity.—God's love for man is an everlasting love. He loved us in Christ before the world began, and purposed from all eternity to save those that believe in Jesus. For God foresaw that the human beings it whom He intended to create would fall into sin. And therefore at the same time that He determined to create man He also determined to redeem him, so "that in the ages to come He might show forth the riches of His grace in His kindness toward us in Christ Jesus" (Eph. 1:4).

God's Love Met the Demands of His Justice.—God is "righteous in all His ways and holy in all His works" (Ps. 145:17). Therefore, much as He loved man, He could not and dared not forgive man's sin without first making provision to satisfy the demands of His own justice. For His justice is demanded man's condemnation. If He would help and save man, He could not do it by being lenient and relaxing the law. For if He had done that, He would no longer be just, and man would have been encouraged in his wickedness. The only way to satisfy justice and the only way to make man a better creature was to execute the punishment in full. But this would have meant the eternal destruction of man. Therefore God determined that He Himself, in the person of His only Son, would suffer the punishment in man's place. This loving purpose, formed from all eternity, was carried out when the fullness of time came. For then "God sent forth His Son, made under the law, to redeem them that were under the law" (Gal. 4:4-5), and "made Him to be sin for us who knew no sin, that we might be made the righteousness of God in Him" (2 Cor. 5:21).

The Greatness of God's Love.—The gift of His only begotten Son for our salvation is the crowning proof of God's love. For in giving us His Son, God not only gave us the greatest gift which it was in His almighty power to bestow, but He gave that gift to men who were His enemies and who deserved His everlasting wrath. "Greater love has no man than this, that a man lay down his life for his friends" (John 15:13). "But God commended His love toward us, in that, while we were yet sinners Christ died for us" (Rom. 5:8). Truly, "God is love" (1 John 4:8).

God's Love Includes All Men.—God desires the salvation of all men. He has "no pleasure in the death of the wicked, but that the wicked turn from His way and live" (Ez. 33:11). He gave His Son for the sins of the whole world, and His gracious plan of salvation is meant for all men without exception. It is this fact which makes Christianity the world religion. For unlike heathen religions, it is not meant for one race, or for one age, or for one part of the earth's surface. And it includes all men of every class and description, whether they be high or low, rich or poor, learned or ignorant, respectable or disreputable. "God would have all men be saved and come to the knowledge of the truth" (1 Tim. 2:4) and He "is not willing that any should perish, but that all should come to repentance'' and live (2 Pet. 3:9).

Therefore, God "now commands all men everywhere to repent" (Acts 17:30). No matter how deeply they may have fallen into sin, God loves them all and is willing to save them all, if they will only repent and believe in Christ. If they believe in Him, then "though their sins be like scarlet, they shall be white as snow; though they be red like crimson, they shall be as wool" (Is. 1:18). For "the blood of Jesus

Christ cleanses us from all sin" (1 John 1:7) and great as our sins may be, God's grace is greater. "Where sin abounded, grace doth much more abound" (Rom. 5:20).

His Love Must be Accepted.—If men would profit by the wonderful love of God, they must believe in Christ. If they do not believe, they receive the grace of God in vain. Only those who are in Christ by faith share in what he has done for men's salvation. Those who do not believe shall be lost

He Bears Long With the Impenitent.—God is gracious and long-suffering, slow to anger and of great mercy. He does not at once send upon men the punishment which they deserve, but withholds it, so that they may be led to repentance by His goodness. He spares no efforts to reclaim them from the error and destruction of their way.

Those Who Despise God's Love are Lost.—If men refuse to repent and believe in Christ, even the love of God, infinite as it is, can do no more for them. They are then irrecoverably lost. The love of God has gone its utmost length in Christ. God cannot do more to save sinful man than He has already done in giving His Son. If this love is despised and rejected, men remain under the wrath of God and are doomed to eternal destruction. For, "how shall we escape if we neglect so great salvation?" (Heb. 2:8). Jesus Christ is "the Way, the Truth and the Life, and no man comes to the Father but by Him" (John 14:6). "Neither is there salvation in any other; for there is none other name under heaven given among men, whereby we must be saved" (Acts 4:18).

CHAPTER VI.
THE OLD TESTAMENT PROPHECIES CONCERNING THE SAVIOR.

During the long centuries that preceded the birth of Christ, God prepared and sustained mankind by the promise, given to a faithful few, that the Savior would certainly come into the world and take our life and flesh upon Him. And the godly men of Old Testament times looked forward with longing to the time when the Messiah should appear.

The Seed of the Woman.—immediately after the Fall, even before He pronounced the sentence of condemnation on man, God promised that a descendant of that very Eve whom the devil had deceived into disobedience, would, at the cost of suffering to Himself, destroy the work of the devil. For God said to the serpent, "I will put enmity between you and the woman, and between your seed and her seed; it shall bruise your head, and you shall bruise his heel" (Gen. 3:15).

The Seed of Abraham.—When Abraham was chosen to be the ancestor of a special people of God, the Lord promised that he should also be the ancestor of the Savior. For God said to Abraham, "In you" and "in your seed shall all the nations of the earth be blessed" (Gen. 28:4).

Of the Tribe of Judah.—Among the sons of Jacob, who were to be the heads of the twelve tribes of Israel, Judah was selected as the one from whom the Messiah or Savior should be descended. The promise of God, given through Jacob on his death-bed, was: "The scepter shall not depart from Judah nor a law-giver from between his feet until Shiloh come; and unto him shall the gathering of the people come" (John 49:10).

The Son of David.—When David had become king over Israel, God gave him the promise, "I will set up thy seed after thee" and " I will establish the throne of your kingdom forever" (2 Sam. 7:12-13). The son of David was a name by which Jesus is was frequently addressed. And because He was the descendant of David, the Jews expected Him to set up an earthly kingdom like that of David.

Prophet, Priest and King.—According to the Old Testament prophecies, the promised Messiah would exercise a threefold office. He would be Prophet, Priest and King. He would be a Prophet and teach the people. For God said to Moses: "I will raise them up a Prophet from among their brethren like unto you, and I will put my words in His mouth, and He shall speak unto them all that I command Him" (Deut. 18:18).

He would be a Priest. For in a Psalm which refers throughout to the coming Savior we are told, that He should be "a Priest forever after the order of Melchizedek" (Ps. 110:4). The priesthood of the Old Testament and its sacrifices for the sins of the people, and especially the High-priesthood, were a type and shadow of Jesus, the great High-priest, and His all-sufficient sacrifice of Himself for the sins of the world.

He would be a King. For the Psalmist said of Him: "He shall have dominion from sea to sea, and from the river to the end of the earth," "His enemies shall lick the dust;" and "all kings shall fall down before Him" (Ps. 72:8-9).

A Substitute for Us.—The coming Savior would be a substitute for men and bear the punishment of their sins in their place. The sacrifice of animals in Old Testament times was accepted as a temporary atonement. But as an animal cannot really take the place of a man, and "it is not possible that the blood of bulls and of goats should take away sins," (Heb. 10:4) the sacrifice of those animals was meant to prefigure and point forward to Christ who would make the true and real sacrifice for sin. Thus the prophet Isaiah, looking forward into the future and beholding the sufferings and death of Jesus as if they had already taken place, said: "He was wounded for our transgressions; He was bruised for our iniquities; the chastisement of our peace was upon Him, and with His stripes we are healed. All we like sheep have gone astray, and the Lord hath laid upon Him the iniquity of us all" (Is. 53:5-6).

Events in His Life Foretold.—Many of the events and circumstances in the Savior's life are accurately foretold in the Old Testament. He should be preceded by a forerunner to prepare His way (Is. 40:3). He would be born of a virgin at Bethlehem (Is. 7:14, Mic. 5:2). Gentiles should come and worship Him, and bring Him gold and incense (Isaiah 60:3, 6). He would give light to those who walk in darkness and who dwell in the land of the shadow of death (Is. 9:2). He would have miraculous power, and open the eyes of the blind, unstop the ears of the deaf, cause the lame to leap as the hart, and the tongue of the dumb to sing (Is. 35:5-6). The kings of the earth would set themselves and the rulers take counsel together against Him (Ps. 2:2). He would ride into Jerusalem as a King, though in poor and lowly state (Zech. 9:9). He would be despised and rejected of men, a man of sorrows and acquainted with grief (Is. 53:3). He would be betrayed by His own friend (Ps. 41:9) for thirty pieces of silver. He would be deserted by His disciples (Zech. 13:7). He would be counted with the malefactors (Is. 53:9). He would die in great agony (Ps. 22:14, 17) while the sun became darkened at noon-day (Amos 8:9). He would pray for His enemies, though reviled by them (Ps. 109:2-4). His bones should not be broken (Ps. 24:20). He would be pierced with a spear (Zech. 12:10). He would be buried with the rich (Is. 53:9). He would rise again from the dead, (Ps. 16:10), ascend into heaven (Ps. 68:18), and sit at the right hand of God (Ps. 110:1).

CHAPTER VII. GOD SENT HIS ONLY SON INTO THE WORLD TO BE OUR SAVIOUR.

When the fullness of time came, God sent the Savior whom He had promised. That Savior is Jesus Christ, the only begotten Son of God, who became man, and lived and suffered and died on earth, that He might redeem us from our sins

Jesus, True Man.– "Conceived by the Holy Ghost and born of the Virgin Mary," Jesus was in every respect a real human being such as we are; only, he was without sin. He had a human body and a human soul. He called Himself the Son of man, and thus indicated that He was true man, yet was distinct from other men by reason of His absolute perfection.

The whole history of His earthly life, as given by the evangelists, records a process of growth and development such as is common to men. He was born, He grew to youth, He increased in wisdom and stature, and reached the age of manhood. He became hungry, thirsty and weary. He was tempted, He was moved with joy, with sorrow and with indignation. He wept, He prayed, He was maltreated, He suffered, and He died. And these things He could not have done, if He had not been true man.

Jesus, True God.–Though He was true man, Jesus was also true God. He is the only begotten Son of the Father. At His baptism and at His transfiguration on the mount, a voice spoke from heaven, and said: "This is My beloved Son, in whom I am well pleased; hear Him" (Matt. 17:5). Divine glory like that of God the Father belonged to Him before the foundation of the world. He is "The Word" who was in the beginning with God and who was God. Before Abraham was, He is. "In Him dwelt all the fullness of the God-head bodily" (Col. 2:9). He is equally God with the Father, and "all men should honor the Son even as they honor the Father" (John 5:23). He and the Father are one (John 10:30). He is in the Father and the Father in Him (John 10:38). He who hath seen Him hath seen the Father (John 14:9).

Jesus, the God-Man.—Jesus Christ is true God and true man in one person. He is God Incarnate, or God become man. For "The Word," that is, the Son of God, "became flesh and dwelt among us" (John 1:14). He is still God and man even now, when He sits at the right hand of God the Father; and He will remain God and man to all eternity.

Why the Son of God Became Man.—This incarnation of the Son of God, or the permanent union of God and man in Jesus Christ, is the greatest miracle of all time. It is a mystery which we cannot understand. But on it our salvation depends. It was necessary that the Son of God should become man in order to save us.

If Jesus had not been both God and man, He could net have become our Savior. For if He had been God only, He could not have put himself in our place under the law of God, nor have suffered and died for our sins. If He had been man only, then, no matter how perfect and holy He might have been, he could not have saved anyone but Himself. But as God and man in one person, He could and did do all that was necessary for our salvation. As a man He perfectly fulfilled the law for us and died for our sins upon the cross. And that which He thus did and suffered for us has infinite worth and power to save, because He is God and man in one person.

Jesus Humbled Himself.—When the Son of God became man, He did not lose any of His divine power and majesty. He was still almighty. He was "the Lord" (John 5:19) of the angels even when He lay as a helpless Infant in the manger at Bethlehem. All power which belonged to Him as God belonged to him also as the God-man, Jesus Christ.

But while He lived on earth as a man among men, Jesus did not use all the power which belonged to Him. He did indeed give men glimpses of His divine majesty in His holy life and in the miracles which He performed. But ordinarily His majesty was veiled. He ate and drank and slept like other men. He was as the lowliest among them. For He was born in poverty, with no room for Him in the inn and He was raised in Nazareth, an obscure village of Galilee. In His manhood's days He had no place to lay His head. In order to pay His taxes on one occasion, he had to send one of His disciples to get the necessary money from the mouth of a fish. And although He could have summoned to His aid more than twelve legions of angels, He permitted Himself to be seized by His enemies, maltreated and put to death, as though He possessed no more power than any other man.

As the God-man, Jesus might have appeared among men in the full splendor of divine glory. But in order to redeem us, it was necessary that He should suffer and die. Therefore as a man, Jesus "humbled Himself and became obedient unto death, even the death of the cross" (Phil. 2:8). Only after His resurrection and ascension did He exercise the full divine power and sovereignty which had belonged to Him all along.

The Names of Jesus.—Various names applied to Jesus in the Scriptures are full of significance, and throw light upon His person and work. The name Emmanuel, applied to Him in the Old and quoted in the New Testament, means "God with us," and points to the union of God and man in Him. The name Jesus, given to Him by the angel, was His personal name, and signifies "He shall save."

The New Testament name Christ and the Old Testament name Messiah are His official title, and both denote the one who is "Anointed" by God for the work of redemption. He is called the Mediator between God and man, because by His sufferings and death He has mediated and made peace between God and us. He is called our Advocate because He pleads for us with the Father. He is called our Great High Priest, because He has once for all He offered Himself as a sacrifice for us, and thus made atonement for our sins.

CHAPTER VIII.
THE MIRACLES OF JESUS.

The land of Palestine rang from end to end with the sound of Christ's miracles. The people were filled with wonder and astonishment by His mighty deeds. No man in all the world's history had displayed such marvelous power. The forces of nature, devils, life, and death lay in subjection at His feet. The prophets of Old Testament times had performed some miracles. But they had done only at rare intervals, and never by virtue of any power inherent in themselves. They prayed to God to do the miracles for them. But Jesus did His miracles by His own power. They were His kingly acts, visible manifestations of His divine glory.

His Mighty Works.—Jesus performed many miracles. Some of them are recorded in the Gospels. But many others which He performed are not recorded. They were so numerous that the evangelists did not undertake to describe them all. His first miracle was the turning of water into wine at the marriage-feast at Cana of Galilee. After that, scarcely a day passed during His public ministry on which He did not perform some miracle, and often great numbers of them. Men came to Him for miraculous healing till far into the night. He healed the sick, the lame, the blind, the deaf, the leprous; cast out devils; caused His disciples to make unprecedented draughts of fishes; stilled the tempest by a word; fed the multitudes with a few loaves and fishes; raised dead persons to life; and rose from the dead Himself on the third day.

Real Miracles.—The reality of Christ's miracles is firmly established by the testimony of His enemies. They hated Him bitterly and were greatly alarmed by the number of people whom His miracles led to believe in Him. If they could have thrown any doubt upon the reality of His miracles and thus counteracted their effect, they unquestionably would have made haste to do so. They sought to attain this end by ascribing His mighty deeds to the power of the devil. And when they failed of their purpose in this way, they determined to put Him to death and thus effectually prevent Him from performing any more miracles. But that His deeds were real miracles, they never once questioned. On the contrary, they freely acknowledged it even when He hung upon the cross; for they sought to embitter His last hours by saying, "He saved others; Himself cannot save himself" (Matt. 27:42).

What the Miracles Were.—The miracles were an unusual operation of the laws of nature. Those laws are God's ordinary way or mode of accomplishing His purposes. They are an expression of His will. But when He sees fit, He can give expression to His will in some other way. In performing His miracles, Jesus showed that, as God and the author of the laws of the world, He is not the slave of those laws, but their master. He accomplished results which startled the people and filled them with amazement, not by breaking the laws of nature, but by directing the operation of the latter in an extraordinary way and through the higher law of His own will.

We ourselves modify the law of gravitation whenever we raise a weight from the ground. We do not abolish or break the law by so doing. The law still exists. But in that particular case its operation is modified by the human will. The more we learn of nature's laws, the more able we become to control them for our own use and to make them our obedient servants. And if we can in some measure control them, Jesus, who is the Son of God, and who not only understands those laws thoroughly but is their author, could do so at will.

Why Jesus Performed Miracles.—Ordinarily God does not modify the regular operation of the laws of nature. But, when the Son of God came into the world as an unknown and humble person, miracles were needed, so that men might know who He was, and that underneath the veil of His humanity they might discover His divinity. Through the miracles He manifested forth His glory and brought men to faith in Him. He established His power in the only way possible then. That way is not needed now, because His divinity is abundantly proved. Even when He was on earth Jesus never performed miracles without a special purpose. He never did them simply to display His powers. He refused to be considered a mere wonder worker.

The miracles of Jesus always had a moral and helpful meaning for the soul. They expressed the good will and saving power of God to men. He did them in order to strengthen, release, or save men's soul. He showed by them that the terrible laws of fate and necessity which seemed to run the world, which appeared resistless, and which make man a mere speck in the immensity of things, can be overcome by the love and power of God. He to whom we pray as our Lord, still has the same power which he exercised in His miracles; and He employs it to control all things so that they "work together for good to them that love Him" (Rom. 8:28).

What the Miracles Proved.—The miracles of Jesus proved that He was the Messiah and Son of God. When John the Baptist sent messengers to Him to inquire, "Are you He that should come or do we look for another?" the answer of Jesus was, "Go and tell John again those things which you hear and see: the blind receive their sight, the lame walk, the lepers are cleansed, the deaf hear, and the poor have the Gospel preached to them" (Matt. 11:3-5). The Old Testament had foretold that when the Messiah came He would do such works; and the miracles proved that Jesus was He. The miracles were extraordinary works which proved the extraordinary claim of Jesus, that He was the Son of God. They bore witness of Him that the Father sent Him. If men were unwilling to believe His words, they were to believe His works. And if they refused to believe on Him after seeing His mighty miracles, they were guilty of the greatest sin, and would fare worse on the Day of Judgment than Sodom and Gomorrah.

Many Believed.—The very first miracle of Jesus produced faith in the hearts of His disciples. Men were convinced that it required far more than human power to do such works. And after He raised Lazarus from the dead, the number of those who believed was so large, that His enemies became alarmed and planned to put Him to death, lest, if they let Him alone, all men would be led to faith through His miracles.

CHAPTER IX.
THE TEACHING OF JESUS

It was part of the Messiah's office as a prophet to teach men. Therefore wherever He went, in Judea, Galilee, Samaria, Jesus taught the people. We find Him teaching in the temple, in the synagogues, on the mountain, by the sea-side, or resting by Jacob's well. Sometimes His pupils consisted of great multitudes; sometimes of only a few disciples; and occasionally of only one person, like Nicodemus or the woman of Samaria.

Jesus the Great Teacher.—In former times God had spoken to men through the prophets, but now He spoke to them by his Son. Coming from the bosom of the Father, Jesus could reveal God's will as no one else could. And He taught with such evident power and authority, that the people were filled with the utmost astonishment, and were convinced that He was a teacher come from God. The teaching of Jesus was the absolute and final truth. It is the climax of God's revelation to men. He told them all that they need to know or will know of God in this world. Even when the Holy Spirit came, whom Jesus sent to guide the disciples into all truth, He simply built on the foundation which Christ had laid, bringing all things which Christ had spoken to their remembrance and making His words clear to them.

What He Taught.— Jesus taught the law of God, and made plain its real meaning. This He did especially in His Sermon on the Mount. He freed the Law from the human traditions with which the scribes and

Pharisees had encumbered it, and showed that it must be fulfilled not only outwardly by deeds, but inwardly in the heart by perfect love to God and man.

But His special work as a teacher was to proclaim the Gospel—the glad tidings of the Kingdom of God which He Himself was now bringing to men. His proclamation may be regarded under two heads: namely, what He taught concerning Himself; and what He taught concerning the Kingdom of God or of Heaven.

Concerning Himself.–Jesus taught, that He is the Son of God who came down from heaven so that men might have eternal life in Him. He would save them by giving His life as a ransom for them. He is "the Way, the Truth, and the Life," and no one can know God or come to the Father except through Him (John 14:6). Repentance and remission of sins are to be preached in His name among all nations. In order to be saved, men must believe on Him. Whoever does not believe will be condemned. He is not only the Savior of men but also their Judge. And He will one day come again to judge and reward them according to their works.

Concerning the Kingdom of God—Jesus taught, that with His coming that kingdom was at hand (Matt. 4:17). It is not a kingdom of this world, outward and visible, but a kingdom in the human heart (Luke 17:20-21). He is its King (Matt. 18:37). Repentance is necessary on the part of all who would become members of kingdom (Matt. 4:17). Those who would belong to it must be humble, and the humblest in it are the greatest (Matt. 18:4). They must be obedient, and not only say "Lord, Lord," but do the will of His "Father in heaven" (Matt. 7:21). He and His subjects are most intimately united like the branch and the vine (John 15:5-6). He not only rules over them, but loves them: they are His friends (John 15:15).

His Parables.—Jesus frequently made use of parables, in order to make His teaching plain. This He did especially in describing the Kingdom of God. By means of illustrations drawn from daily life, He shows how that kingdom grow externally and internally till it extends over the whole world, and exerts a sacred influence over the whole race; how anxiously God desires that men should belong to it; how foolishly some despise its offers of grace; its subjects are gathered into it; and how in it the good and the bad are found side by side in this world.

He also shows how its subjects must, like a tree, bear fruit or be destroyed; how they must forgive others in order to retain the forgiveness of God themselves; and how they should show mercy to the needy. He warns them not to set their heart on the things of this world; so urges them to be faithful in serving Him; and bids them look for a reward of grace and not of merit. He shows them how the godly and the ungodly respectively fare in the next world; warns them of the suddenness with which He will come to judge the world; and bids them watch and be always ready, because they "know not the day nor the hour in which the Son of man will come" (Matt. 25:13).

His Moral Precepts.—Jesus intends that men shall be saved only by faith in Him. But at the same time, the character and conduct of those who believe in Him is to bear witness to their faith. They are to let their light shine before men. To this end He has given many precepts, showing what kind of people his followers should be in heart and life. They should aim at a far higher standard of moral excellence than other men. They are to love God above all things and their neighbor as themselves.

In his dealings with his fellow men, the Christian is to follow the Golden Rule of doing to others as he would have others do to him. He should be uniformly kind in his treatment of them, be wholly free from ill-will or animosity against any one, and never be guilty of unkind words. If he has wronged any one, he should be ready to acknowledge his fault and make amends. If others have offended or injured him, he must be ready to forgive. He must not take revenge, but return good for evil, and love even his enemies. He should be kind and charitable in his judgment and opinion of other people; he should not pick out their faults and hold them up to view, but be concerned to overcome his own. He should be pure and chaste in mind and heart as well as in deed. He should be careful in his speech, so as not only to avoid profanity but also all useless and idle words. He should be ready to help everyone that is in distress, but when he has done so, he should not boast or make a show. Religious life is to be sincere and earnest, but quiet and unostentatious, free from unbelieving care and worry, and trustful of God's Fatherly care. And he should resolutely cut loose from everything that hinders him from securing his own salvation or performing God's will.

CHAPTER X.
THE HOLY LIFE OF JESUS.

In the midst of a world of sinful men, Jesus lived a sinless and holy life. He is the only human being who ever fulfilled God's law perfectly by loving God above all things and His neighbor as Himself.

The Holiness of Jesus.—Having God alone for His Father, Jesus was free from that inborn sinfulness and depravity of the heart which all other men inherit in consequence of the Fall into sin. And during His entire life He "did no sin, neither was guile found in His mouth" (1 Pet. 2:22). He was "the Holy and Just" One (Acts 3:14). He was holy as God Himself is holy; for He was "the brightness of God's glory and the express image of His person" (Heb. 1:3). He was "holy, harmless, undefiled and separate from sinners," (Heb. 7:26) and was "without blemish or spot" (1 Pet. 1:19).

Tempted, Yet Without Sin.—Being true man, it was possible for Jesus to be tempted. And He was "in all points tempted like as we are." Yet He remained without sin (Heb. 4:15). He never yielded to temptation, no matter how strong or cunning or long-continued were Satan's assaults. His bitterest enemies could not point out a single sin in Him, though they would have been only too glad to do so if they could. He taught His disciples to pray, "Forgive us our sins" (Luke 11:4). But, although He Himself often prayed, He never asked for the forgiveness of His own sins. He had none to be forgiven. And when He died, it was for our sins, and not for any which He Himself had committed.

Jesus Perfectly Fulfilled God's Law:

1. Toward God.—Jesus loved God with all His heart and with all His soul and with all His mind. At twelve years of age, He was found in the temple "about His Father's business" (Luke 2:49). And throughout His whole life He sought to do "not His own will, but the will of His Father who sent Him" (John 5:30). So completely did He do that will, that at the end of His days He could say to His Father, "I have glorified you on earth; I have finished the work which you gave me to do" (John 17:4). He preferred to worship and serve God in lowliness and humility, rather than receive "the kingdoms of the world and the glory of them" (Matt. 4:8-16). Though the path in which God's will led Him was one of intense suffering, He cheerfully walked in it, and "was obedient unto death, even the death of the cross" (Phil. 2:8).

2. *Toward Man.*—Jesus loved men with a perfect love. This is manifest from what He did and suffered for them. He came among them "not to be ministered unto but to minister, and to give His life a ransom for many" (Matt. 20:28). He was moved with pity for men's bodily needs and diseases. He never refused to help them, even if they came to Him when He was weary with a long day's work. The very sight of suffering or need appealed to Him for help. He frequently helped men without being directly besought to do so. And He did not refrain from helping them, even when He knew that His act of kindness would be misconstrued by His enemies.

He was moved with compassion especially for men's souls. He pitied "the multitudes, because they were as sheep without a shepherd" (Matt. 9:36). And He willingly endured the greatest sufferings and died the shameful death of the cross, in order that He might redeem them from their sinful and lost condition. His love included the whole human race; for He died for all and commanded His Gospel to be preached to all. It included the lowest, the most despised, and the outcast among men; for He received the publicans and sinners, and ate with them. He loved even His bitterest enemies; for He not only never took revenge upon them, but prayed for them while they nailed Him to the cross.

What His Holy Life Proves.—No mere man could have lived the holy life of Jesus, any more than a mere man could have performed His miracles. For since the Fall into sin all other men have been born with a sinful heart and a natural inclination to evil. The best men among the heathen sink infinitely below the holiness of Jesus. The prophets of Old Testament times, though they led comparatively holy lives, had their faults and shortcomings. And the best of Christians, though they derive strength from Christ Himself to lead new lives of holiness, are very far removed from His perfection. He alone was absolutely without sin. And His holiness proves that He is what He claimed to be, the Son of God.

An Example for Us.—In leading a life of perfect love to God and man, Jesus has "left us an example that we should follow His steps" (1 Pet. 2:21). He Himself kept the commandments which He gave us, and thus showed us how we ought to keep them. We are to take His "yoke upon us and learn" of Him (Matt. 11:21). If we abide in Him, we are "to walk even as He walked" and love one another even as He loved us (1 John 2:6, John 13:34).

He Fulfilled the Law for Us.—The chief significance of Christ's holy life lies in the fact, that by it He perfectly obeyed the law of God for us. The fulfillment of that law entitles the one who fulfills it to receive a reward. Jesus did not need that reward for Himself, because He is the Son of God and from eternity possesses all glory. We need it, but cannot earn it. Therefore Jesus placed Himself under the law and won the reward for us. We need not only to have our sins taken away, but also to obtain a righteousness that will fit us for heaven. By his complete and perfect obedience to God's law Jesus has acquired that righteousness. And He bestows it upon all who believe on Him. As by Adam's disobedience many were made sinners, so by the obedience of Christ many are made righteous. For Christ is "made unto us wisdom and righteousness and sanctification and redemption" (1 Cor. 1:30).

CHAPTER XI.
THE SIGNIFICANCE OF CHRIST'S SUFFERINGS AND DEATH.

Jesus suffered and died in order that He might bear the punishment and make amends for the sins of the whole world.

Sin Must Be Atoned For.—We all know in our best selves, that when an injury or a wrong has been done, the offender cannot expect to have things made right again until he has made restitution for the injury and suffered punishment for the wrong. Without such a demand for restitution and punishment, all fairness and justice in men's dealings with one another would die away. If this is a fact even in men's relations with one another, how much more must it be a fact in the dealings of a holy, just and impartial God with men. The human heart has always felt that sin demands punishment and cannot be forgiven until an expiation or atonement has been made. This conviction is confirmed by the Scriptures. For without shedding of blood there can be no remission of sins.

In the Old Testament God tried to educate Israel up to the deep conviction of the necessity of such restitution, punishment and expiation, by commanding them to make sin offerings, and especially a yearly atonement by the high priest. These offerings of the Israelites were not sufficient to make atonement for men's sins. They were only figurative, and pointed forward to the real expiation which would be by Christ the Savior. But they were accepted by God. God meanwhile, in view of the atonement which Christ Heb. is the Great High Priest, and the real sacrifice for sin.

What Jesus Suffered.—The sufferings of Jesus for us extended over the entire period of His earthly life. He endured all the trials and hardships which are common to men. In addition to that, He suffered the constant persecution of His enemies. And as a holy and perfect being, He necessarily experienced the greatest mental and spiritual anguish from His contact and identification with a sinful and guilty world. But the climax of His sufferings was reached at the end of His life, in His agony in the garden of Gethsemane, His seizure by His enemies, His trial, maltreatment and condemnation by the Jewish council and Roman governor, and His shameful death upon the cross.

Jesus Suffered and Died Voluntarily.—The death of Jesus was not an unforeseen accident which spoiled all His plans. It was the very object for which He had come into the world. It took place in accordance with God's eternal purpose and with Christ's own foreknowledge. He told His disciples of His approaching sufferings, and voluntarily went forward to endure them. No man could take His life from Him. He laid it down of Himself. The multitudes who came out by night to seize Him could not have done so if He had been unwilling. But He permitted them to capture Him and lead Him away to trial and death, in order that He might suffer all that we deserved by our sins.

Why Jesus Suffered and Died.—The death of Jesus was not intended simply to show us how much God loves us, or how much He hates sin. It was not meant to be merely an example of the patience which we should exercise in suffering, or to show us how nobly and gloriously a man may and should meet even an unjust death. It does do these things. But it does much more. Its chief significance lies in the fact that it was an atonement for our sins. He offered Himself as a sacrifice for our guilt, and thus satisfied the demands of God's justice. "He was wounded for our transgressions, He was bruised for our iniquities" (Is. 53:5). He put Himself in our place, and endured the punishment which we deserved. His sufferings were vicarious.

His Death was Sufficient for All.—The death of Jesus is full atonement for the sins of the whole world. His sufferings and death are the equal of the sufferings and death of all. He not only suffered in our place, but He suffered all that we deserved. We cannot fully realize the extremity of Christ's sufferings. We see something of their greatness, however, when we behold Him in the garden of Gethsemane wrestling with God in prayer till the sweat rolled from His brow like great drops of blood; when we listen to His prayer, "Father, if it be possible, let this cup pass from Me" (Matt. 26:39); and when we hear His agonized cry on the cross, "My God, My God, why have you forsaken Me?" (Matt. 24:46). The whole burden of the world's guilt and of God's wrath against the world's sin lay upon Jesus. And the burden was so great, that even He, supported as He was by all the strength which belonged to Him as the God-man, could scarcely endure it. An eternity of human woe and torment was compressed within the limits of His sufferings and death.

Therefore His death is a full and complete atonement for our sins. He "has redeemed us from the curse of the law, being made a curse for us" (Gal. 3:13). By "His own blood He has obtained eternal redemption for us," having once for all put away sin by the sacrifice of Himself (Heb. 9:26).

God Reconciled.—As the result of the sufferings and death of Christ, God is reconciled to man. For "God was in Christ, reconciling the world unto Himself, not imputing their trespasses unto them" (2 Cor. 5:19). The needs of justice are now fully satisfied, and God is free to forgive sins for Christ's sake without ceasing to be a just and holy God. Indeed, now that all the requirements of the law have been met by Christ, God's justice itself unites with His love in bestowing forgiveness upon the believer. All men may, if they will, find forgiveness of sins through Christ. For God "has made peace through the blood of His cross, by Him to reconcile all things unto Himself" (Col. 1:20).

The Atonement Made Ours by Faith.—In order to profit by what Christ has done, we must accept it by faith. God does not force salvation upon the unwilling. But if men believe in Christ, then God regards and treats them as if they themselves had done all that Christ has done for them. He imputes Christ's righteousness to them. They are justified, that is, counted righteous for Christ's sake. For "being justified by faith, we have peace with God through our Lord Jesus Christ" (Rom. 5:21), and "shall be saved from wrath through Him" (Rom. 5:9).

CHAPTER XII. THE BIBLE TEACHING OF THE RESURRECTION OF JESUS.

The Savior always had taught that He was the Resurrection and the Life. As the Son of God who is alive forevermore and is the same yesterday, today and forever, and as the Prince of Life who raised others from the dead, Jesus could not remain in the grave. In accordance with the Old Testament prophecies and with his own predictions, He rose from the dead on the third day. He "had power to lay down His life, and power to take it again" (John 10:18).

A Real Return From Death to Life.—As the death of Jesus was not a seeming but an actual death like that of any other man who dies, so His resurrection was a real return from death to life. He reappeared to His disciples, not as a spirit, but with the same body which had been put to death on the cross. His body could be touched and felt, and had flesh and bones just as any other body has showed plainly the marks made by the nails in His hands and feet. But it possessed new properties and powers. It was no longer subject to the same limitations as our body now is. Jesus could appear and disappear at will, and could pass through closed doors. His body was a transformed and glorified body, such as ours also shall be after our resurrection.

The Resurrection a Fact.—The disciples had been so disheartened by the crucifixion, that they had practically lost faith in Jesus as the Messiah, and had forgotten His promise to rise again from the dead. They never for a moment thought of deceiving the people, as the Pharisees thought they might, by stealing the body of Jesus and then telling the people that He had risen. But if they had thought of it, they could not have done so, because the chief priests and Pharisees sealed His sepulchre, and set a guard of soldiers before it.

The resurrection of Jesus is a fact. The strongest proof of this fact is that the disciples themselves were so skeptical about it, and so set in their notion of its impossibility, that they never would have believed it, if they had not been obliged to do so by the evidence of their own eyes. They demanded the strongest and most abundant proofs before they were willing to believe. When they first were told that Jesus had risen, the words of those who brought the news "seemed to them idle tales, and they believed them not" (Luke 24:11). Thomas, one of the twelve, even went so far as to declare, "Except I shall see in His hands the print of the nails, and put my finger into the print of the nails, and thrust my hand into His side, I will not believe." But when Jesus showed Him his hands and His side, even Thomas was convinced and cried out, "My Lord and my God" (John 30:25-26).

Jesus Appeared Often to His Disciples.—Jesus tarried on the earth forty days after He rose from the dead. And during this time He gave His disciples so many and such plain proofs of His resurrection, that, slow as they were to believe, their doubts were all removed. The women who went to His grave on Easter morning found it empty, and were told by the angel, "He is risen, He is not here" (John 20:14-16). Mary saw Him in the garden, and mistook Him for the gardener until He called her by name. He was seen by Peter, by the two disciples on the way to Emmaus, and twice by the apostles as they were gathered together. He appeared to several of His disciples as they were fishing on the sea of Tiberias. He was seen by more than five hundred disciples at once. After that He was seen by

James, and then by all the apostles. He was accompanied by the disciples out to Mount Olivet, where He ascended into heaven before their eyes. And after His ascension He was seen also by Paul.

A Great Change in the Apostles.—These appearances of our Lord made the disciples so certain of His resurrection that a great change took place in them all. Instead of being discouraged and dismayed as they had been before, the twelve now became filled with joyful confidence, and, having received the gift of the Holy Ghost, went forth everywhere preaching the Gospel of the crucified and risen Savior. And Paul, who had been a bitter persecutor of the Christians, became a preacher of the Gospel and underwent the greatest labors, trials and sufferings for Christ's sake. Nothing but the unalterable conviction that Jesus had indeed risen from the dead and now reigns in heaven can account for so marvelous a transformation.

The Importance of the Resurrection.—When the apostles chose a man to take the place of Judas Iscariot among them, they were careful to select one who had been a witness of the resurrection. And when they went forth to proclaim the Gospel, they based their preaching on the fact that Jesus had risen from the dead. Without the resurrection, they could not have persuaded men to believe on Jesus. For if He had not risen, He would have been simply a man, even though a holy man who had been unjustly put to death. But His resurrection proves that He is the Son of God. No mere man ever did or could rise from the dead and ascend into heaven as Jesus did. God would not have raised up from the dead one who said He was the Son of God, if He had not been what He claimed. The voice from heaven at His baptism had declared and His miracles, teaching and holy life had shown that He was the Son of God. And now the resurrection confirmed and sealed all that had been said and done. Jesus could die as other men die, but He could not as God's "Holy One see corruption" (Acts 2:24-31). On the contrary, He "was declared to be the Son of God with power by His resurrection from the dead" (Rom. 1:4).

A Proof of Christ's Atonement.—The resurrection proves that the sacrifice which Jesus made for us on the cross satisfied in full the demands of God's justice. He suffered all that we deserved by our sins. And the resurrection is God's testimony that He has done so. If His sacrifice had not been sufficient, Jesus would have remained in the power of death. But He arose from the dead, and thus proved that His atonement is complete and our ransom fully paid. "He was delivered for our offences, and rose again for our justification" (Rom. 4:25). He has conquered sin and death and hell for us, and has "brought life and immortality to light" (2 Tim. 1:10).

A Proof of Our Resurrection.—As surely as Christ rose from the dead, so surely will there be also a resurrection of all the dead. "God who raised up Jesus from the dead will also raise up us" (1 Cor. 6:14). The hour is coming in which all that are in the graves shall hear the voice of Jesus and shall come forth; they that have done good, unto the resurrection of life; and they that have done evil, unto the resurrection of damnation (1 Cor. 6:14).

Through the resurrection of Jesus, death has lost its terrors for the believers. It is for them only a sleep from which they shall one day awake at His word. Then He will change their "vile body, that it may be fashioned like unto His own glorious body, according to the working whereby He is able to subdue all things unto Himself" (Phil. 3:21).

CHAPTER XIII.
THE SIGNIFICANCE OF CHRIST'S ASCENSION INTO HEAVEN. HIS SITTING AT THE RIGHT HAND OF THE FATHER.

Jesus remained on the earth forty days after His resurrection, in order to give His disciples "infallible proofs" that He was risen. Then He went with them to Mount Olivet, and, while they beheld, "He was received up into heaven and sat on the right hand of God" (Mark 16:19).

Christ Exalted.—Jesus had "humbled Himself and become obedient unto death, even the death of the cross" (Phil. 2:8), in order that by so doing He might redeem men from destruction. Therefore "God also hath highly exalted Him, and given Him a name that is above every name: that at the name of Jesus every knee should bow, of things in heaven, and things in earth, and things under the earth; and that every tongue should confess that Jesus Christ is Lord, to the glory of God the Father" (Phil. 2:9-11). The work which Jesus had come into the world to do was completed. And now He returned to that heaven from which He had come, and occupied the place which belonged to Him as the Son of God. The necessity for His humiliation being past, His exaltation took place.

Exalted as Man.—As God, Jesus is unchangeable, "the same yesterday, today and forever" (Heb. 13:8), and could neither be humiliated nor exalted. But as man He had humbled Himself and refrained from the full use of the power which belonged to Him. As man therefore He was now exalted. He Himself told His disciples immediately before His ascension, "All power is given to me in heaven and on earth" (Matt. 28:18). And He ascended into heaven to exercise that power.

At the Right Hand of God.—Jesus now sits at the right hand of God, that is to say, at the right hand of God's power. For God is a Spirit, and therefore has neither a right nor a left hand. But since man's chief strength usually lies in his right hand or arm, we speak of God's power as His right hand.

As the Son of God, Christ sat on the right hand of God from all eternity. He is equally God with the Father and the Holy Spirit, sharing in all the power and majesty of God. But as man He did not sit at the right hand of God till after the ascension. Then it was that Jesus, as the God-man, assumed the sovereignty over heaven and earth. For the Father "set Him at His own right hand in the heavenly places, far above all principality, and power, and might, and dominion, and every name that is named, not only in this world, but also in that which is to come," and "hath put all things under His feet" (Eph. 1:20-22). "Angels, authorities and powers have been made subject unto Him" (1 Pet. 3:22).

Christ Still God and Man.—Jesus did not cease to be man when he ascended into Heaven and sat on the right hand of the Father. It was only as man that He needed to be or could be exalted. He is therefore still man as well as God now when He sits at the right hand of God, just as He was when He dwelt on the earth. A true human being such as we are, only without sin, and glorified, now reigns over all the universe in the person of Jesus Christ, the God-man.

Jesus Pleads for Us.—Sitting at the right hand of God, Jesus is our Intercessor. He pleads for us with the Father. He shed His blood for the remission of our sins.

And He holds up between us and His Father the merit and righteousness which He acquired for us by His holy life and innocent death. He makes intercession for us continually. We have in Christ a great High Priest who is passed into the heavens—not a High Priest who "cannot be touched with the feeling of our infirmities, but who was Himself tempted in all points like as we are, yet without sin" (Heb. 4:14). He knows and feels all that we need; for He Himself is also man. As in Old Testament times the high priest entered into God's presence and interceded for the people, so Christ, who is ever in God's presence, pleads for us. The Father Himself loves us and is disposed to grant us His grace and favor. Much more will He grant it to us, when His only Son, who shed His blood for us, intercedes for us. We are therefore in Christ's name to "come boldly to the throne of grace, that we may obtain mercy, and find grace to help in time of need" (Heb. 4:16).

He Rules Over Us.—Sitting at the right hand of God, Jesus is King and Lord over all. The Father has given all things into His hands. "And He must reign till He hath put all enemies under His feet" (1 Cor. 15:25). His kingdom is a threefold one: a kingdom of power, of grace and of glory.

His Kingdom of Power includes all things and all men. For He is God over all, and holds dominion over the whole universe. He rules over all men, good or bad, over good and bad angels, and over every other creature. All things have been "put in subjection under His feet" (Heb. 2:8). He is "the King of kings and Lord of Lords," to whom belongs "honor and power everlasting" (1 Tim. 6:15-16).

His Kingdom of Grace includes all the believers while they are in this world. In this kingdom, which is called His Church, He bestows upon the believers all the blessings which He has acquired by His obedience and sufferings. By means of the Word of God and the sacraments He gathers, governs, preserves and defends them as His own. He bestows upon them all things that they need in body and soul, and is with them "always, even unto the end of the world" (Matt. 28:20).

His Kingdom of Glory includes the good angels and all those men who have died in the faith. The kingdom of grace shall be merged completely into the kingdom of glory at the end of the world. At that time Christ will raise the dead to life. And then those believers whom He has raised from the dead as well as the believers who are yet alive at the end of the world shall be taken by Christ unto Himself in heaven, that where He is "there they may be also" (John 17:24). There they shall live and reign with Him in glory forever.

CHAPTER XIV.
THE HOLY SPIRIT AND THE NEW BIRTH WHICH HE PRODUCES IN MAN.

The Holy Spirit, or the Holy Ghost, is the third person of the Holy Trinity. He proceeds from the Father and the Son, and with the Father and the Son together is worshipped and glorified" (Nicene Creed). He is true God as well as the Father and the Son, and equal to them in glory and majesty.

When Jesus sent forth His disciples to baptize all nations, He told them to do so "in the name of the Father and of the Son and of the Holy Ghost" (Matt. 28:29). In the apostolic benediction which reads, "The grace of our Lord Jesus Christ, the love of God, and the communion of the Holy Ghost be with you all" (2 Cor. 13:14), the Holy Spirit is put on a level with the Father and the Son. He is called in the Scriptures Jehovah, Lord and God. He is spoken of as eternal, omnipotent, omniscient and omnipresent. He has share in the creation and preservation of the world. He instructed the prophets and teachers of old, and inspired the writing of the Bible. And the entire work of sanctification, or applying to men's souls the redemption of Jesus, is ascribed to Him.

A Person.—The Holy Spirit is not merely a power or energy which God supplies, but is a Person. He is, indeed, spoken of in some passages of Scripture as the Spirit of God and the Spirit of Christ; and this Spirit of God and Spirit of Christ, we are told, should dwell in the believers. But it is the third person of the Holy Trinity that is meant, And not simply a mind or disposition such as God wants us to have. The outpouring of the Holy Ghost on the day of Pentecost was not simply a filling of the human spirit of the apostles with enlightenment, courage and zeal in the cause of the Savior, but the coming of a divine person into their hearts.

Acts such as only a person can do are ascribed to the Holy Spirit. He strives with sinners, reproves the world, testifies of Christ, teaches, guides and comforts the believers, helps their infirmities, and sanctifies them. He is as truly a person as the Father or the Son.

His Work.—The work which the Holy Ghost does in us is as necessary for our salvation as the work which Christ has done for us. Christ has indeed died for all men, and made it possible for all men to be saved if they will. When He was about to die on the cross, He said, "It is finished" (John 19:30). And so it was. The holy life had been lived and the punishment for sin endured. Justice was satisfied, and the forgiving love of God could be freely exercised. But men must be made willing and able to accept salvation. They must be brought to faith. Without faith they would perish in spite of all that Christ has done for them.

It is the work of the Holy Spirit to create this faith in men. In doing so, He produces a great and radical change in the soul. This change is called in the Scriptures a new birth or regeneration.

Why the New Birth is Necessary.—A new birth is necessary in man, because he is by nature spiritually dead. Sin has cut him off from the spiritual life which he would otherwise have drawn from God. He is "dead in trespasses and sins" (Eph. 2:1). Therefore he has no power of his own to discern spiritual things, to recognize his lost condition, to repent of his sins, or to believe in Christ his Savior. He must be born again; not physically, indeed, but spiritually. Unless he is born again, he cannot see nor enter into the kingdom of God. A new spiritual life must be created in him, in order that he may be able to appropriate to himself by faith "the redemption that is in Christ Jesus" (Rom. 3:24).

No one but God can produce this new life. It is God that must work "in us both to will and to do of His good pleasure" (Phil. 2:13). "No man can say that Jesus is the Lord, but by the Holy Ghost" (1 Cor. 12:3). Those in whom this new life has been wrought are born of God and born of the Spirit. They are no longer children of wrath as they were by nature, but have become children of God and heirs of everlasting life.

The Means.—In order to accomplish results, men use means. The scholar writes with his pen, the mechanic works with his tools, the manufacturer uses his machines. God Himself works through means in the realm of nature. He illumines and warms the earth by means of the sun, and waters it by means of the rain. It is natural, therefore, that the Holy Spirit should use means in order to produce and sustain in men the new spiritual life. The means which He uses are the Word of God and the Sacraments. They are called the Means of Grace, because they are the means or channels through which the Holy Spirit brings God's grace to our hearts. Through them he awakens men to a knowledge of their sin, leads them to repentance and faith, and strengthens and preserves them in the faith to the end of their life.

The Word of God.—The chief means through which the Holy Spirit works in men's hearts is the Word of God. Even in the sacraments, Baptism and the Lord's Supper, it is the Word of God, with its command and promise, that gives them their value. It is principally through the Word of God, with its Law and its Gospel, which He Himself has inspired, that the Holy Spirit accomplishes His work He is always in that Word, and through it not only tells men what to do but gives them the power to do it. "The Word of God is quick and powerful and sharper than any two-edged sword" (Heb. 4:12). "It is the power of God unto salvation to everyone that believeth" (Rom. 1:16). Through the Holy Spirit who constantly dwells in it, the Word of God regenerates, converts, renews, and sanctifies all who do not wilfully resist its power.

Baptism.—Infants, being by nature sinful, need to be born again as well as adults. But as they are not yet old enough to hear and understand God's Word, the Holy Spirit implants the new life in them through Baptism; for baptism is "a washing of regeneration and renewal by the Holy Ghost" (Tit. 3:5). The new life thus implanted in infancy is nourished and strengthened in after years by the Word of God.

Human Instruments.—The Holy Spirit makes use of men as His instruments in accomplishing His purpose in the soul. For this reason He founded the Christian Church and committed to it the preaching of the Word of God and the administration of the sacraments. Christians thus become laborers together with God. And as workers together with Him, they beseech men not to receive the grace of God in vain. Knowing the terror of the Lord and His anger against sin, they persuade men to believe in Christ and be saved.

CHAPTER XV. HOW THE HOLY SPIRIT CONVERTS MEN OR BRINGS THEM TO FAITH.

All who are not living a life of faith, but are impenitent and unbelieving, need to be converted or turned in faith to Christ. This includes all those who have not as infants been regenerated by the Holy Spirit in baptism, as well as all those who have fallen from their baptismal grace into sin and unbelief.

What Conversion Is.—Regarded from the divine side, the change which takes place in man when he is brought to faith is called the new birth or regeneration, because it is the implanting of a new spiritual life in him by the Holy Spirit. Regarded from the human side, the change is called conversion, because it is a converting or turning away of man from sin and self to righteousness and God.

Repentance.—The word Repentance is frequently used to express the same meaning as conversion. In its narrow sense it means sorrow for sin, like the words penitence or contrition. But in its wider sense it includes faith as well as penitence. It is frequently used in this wider sense in the Bible, and means a change of mind, a turning away of the heart from sin to God. Thus used, the term is essentially synonymous with conversion.

True repentance always leads to faith. Sorrow for sin which does not lead to faith is not repentance but remorse, and often ends in despair. The sorrow of Peter after he denied his Lord was repentance; that of Judas after he betrayed Christ was remorse.

The Holy Spirit Calls Men.—In order that men may be converted from their sins to faith in Christ, the Holy Spirit calls them through the Gospel. He has caused the Word of God to be written and causes it to be continually proclaimed for the purpose of thus making known to men the grace of God in Christ and inviting them to share in it. He bids them believe in Christ and be saved. They are to come and partake freely of God's grace; for all things are now ready. Everything that is necessary for their salvation has been done, and God wants them all to believe in Christ and be saved.

He Enlightens Them.—"Having the understanding darkened and being alienated from the life of God through the ignorance that is in them" (Eph. 4:18), men do not, as they are by nature, realize their lost condition and their need of salvation. Therefore the Holy Spirit enlightens them through the law and the Gospel, showing them the peril of their sinful state and the goodness of God which desires to save them from it.

Through the Law, He reveals to them not only what they ought to do, but also the guilt which they have incurred and the punishment which they have deserved by not doing what they should. He thus makes plain to them that they must perish unless they find a way of escape.

Through the Gospel, He shows them God's infinite love and mercy, how the Son of God became man and lived on earth and suffered and died to redeem them, and how willing God is to pardon them, if they will only repent of their sins and believe in Christ their Savior.

He Gives Power to Obey the Call.—Being dead in trespasses and sins, men have no power to obey the call of the Gospel. But the Holy Spirit is always in the Word of God; and through that Word, He not only tells them to believe, but also enables them to do so. When the dead young man at Nain was told by Jesus to arise, he had no power to hear or obey the Savior's command. He was dead; and a dead person has no power to do anything. Yet dead though he was, that young man heard and obeyed the command of the Lord. He did so because the word which Christ spoke was the Word of God and brought with it the power which he needed. Just so it is with the Gospel and its command to repent and be saved. It comes to men who are spiritually dead; but it brings to them the power to obey, because it is the Word of God.

He Leads Them to Repentance.—If men do not wilfully resist His grace, the Holy Spirit leads them to repentance. He teaches them to compare themselves with the requirements of God's holy law, and thus shows them how sinful and guilty they are in God's sight, fills their heart with sincere sorrow for their sins, with a hatred of sin, and with a longing to be forgiven.

He Leads Them to Faith.—Having filled men's hearts with an earnest desire for salvation, the Holy Spirit holds up Christ before them as the Savior through whom they may abundantly receive the remission of their sins. He shows them what Christ has done and suffered to redeem them, and how willing God is to pardon them for Christ's sake. Thus He prevails on them to trust in Christ and to believe with sure confidence that God has forgiven them all their sins.

Who is Converted.—It is not necessary that a Christian should be able to point to the day and hour of his conversion. Some can do so; but many others cannot. Baptized in infancy and brought up in the fear of God, the believing child of God has always lived in a regenerate state, repenting of his sins and believing in Christ. He needs no additional conversion, but has been a saved member of Christ's Church ever since he was baptized.

Among the apostles of Jesus none but Paul could point to the exact time of his conversion. The faith of the others was a matter of very gradual growth. Little by little their minds were opened to the truth and their faith developed till, after the outpouring of the Holy Spirit, it broke forth into triumphant confidence in Him. But they believed in Christ long before that time. So it is with many others. Their conversion has been gradual, not sudden and violent; and they cannot, therefore, point to the exact time when it took place. The important question is not, when were we converted, but are we in a converted state: are we penitent and believing.

Wilful Resistance.—When the Holy Spirit calls men, He gives them power to repent. But His work may be resisted. Men may and often do refuse to obey the Gospel. They harden their hearts in their sins. By so doing, they grieve the Holy Spirit. He is patient and comes to their hearts again and again. But if they persist in hardening themselves against Him, He will finally stay away. Men dare not, like Felix, wait for a convenient season. Such a season will never come. It will never be convenient but always a trial to the flesh to turn away from sin. We must obey the call of the Gospel whenever it comes to us. Those who refuse to repent when the Spirit moves them to do so may find at last no place for repentance, though they seek it carefully with tears. Now is the accepted time, now is the day of salvation, tomorrow it may be too late.

Death-Bed Repentance.—Repentance or conversion even in the last hour, if sincere, saves men. This is proved by the example of the thief on the cross. But men dare not deliberately postpone repentance till that time. They may not have time to repent then. They may not be able to repent then, even if they want to do so. The power to repent must come from God. And if the Holy Spirit has been deliberately sent away during the days of health, He may not come to their hearts in their last hour, but let them die in their sins. Out of the many wicked men described in the Bible, the thief on the cross is the only one of whom we are told that he repented in the last hour and was saved. How many on the other hand died as they had lived, in sin and guilt! One example of repentance at the last hour is given to us, in order that no one may despair if he truly repents; but only one, so that no one may deliberately and presumptuously postpone repentance till the last hour.

CHAPTER XVI.
WHAT FAITH IS.

Without faith man cannot be saved. The promise of salvation is given only to those who believe. "He that believeth is not condemned; but he that believeth not is condemned already, because he hath not believed on the only begotten Son of God" (John 3:18).

All Men Exercise Faith.—In matters of this world all men exercise faith. A child lives by faith in its mother. A business man lives by faith that he will have custom, that his goods will arrive at a certain time, that his bank will not fail, that his customers will pay him. We all have faith in other men. We must take their word for many things which we cannot see ourselves. We believe that they will have for sale what we need to buy in order to live. When we travel we depend on others to have the train on hand at the appointed time, and we trust the engineer, the switchman and the despatcher with our lives. We exercise faith in others every day of our life. We depend on them to fulfil their promises and their obligations. If men refuse to believe in God, they refuse to place in Him as much trust as they put in their fellow men.

A Matter of the Heart.—Without faith it is impossible to please God. It is important, therefore, to know what true faith is. It is not a mere intellectual belief in the existence of God or of the truth of the facts recorded in the Bible. Many impenitent men and even the devils themselves have that kind of faith. But such belief is not faith in the Christian sense. Faith is not only a matter of the head, but of the heart.

Based on Knowledge.—Though knowledge of the facts of the Gospel is by no means all that is necessary, knowledge is an essential part of faith. Men must first have knowledge of Christ and of what He has done for them, before they can believe on Him as their Savior. This is why Christ commanded His disciples to go into all the world and preach the Gospel to every creature; why the Holy Spirit by inspiring the Bible provided men with a correct record of all that Christ has done for us; and why the Christian Church in obedience to Christ's command preaches the Gospel at home and sends forth her missionaries to preach it to the heathen.

Belief of the Facts.—We must not only know the facts of the Gospel, but believe them to be true. Faith implies the taking of another's word for the truth of a statement. In this case it is the taking of God's word; for the Bible is His Word. Thus Abraham took God's word and staggered not at His promise, however unlikely its fulfilment seemed from the human standpoint, but was strong in the faith, nothing doubting but that what God had promised He was also able to perform. Faith is accepting the truth of things not seen. And blessed are they who have not seen and yet believe.

Trust in Christ.—The chief part of faith, however, is trust in the merit and righteousness of Christ. We must not only believe that Jesus is the Son of God and that He died for the sins of men, but believe that He died for us, and that God for His sake forgives us all our sins. Faith is an individual appropriation of what Christ has done. It believes that through His redemption salvation is really and actually ours. It is trust; it is confidence. It is believing for a certainty and without doubt that our sins are all washed away by Christ's precious blood. It is to say with St. Paul, "The Son of God loved me and gave Himself for me" (Gal. 2:20). It is taking God's word as true and as meaning us when He promises for Christ's sake to forgive our sins and make us heirs of eternal life.

It Must be Preceded by Repentance.—There can be no true and saving faith in Christ, unless there first be true repentance for sin. The promise of forgiveness is not made to the impenitent but only to those who sincerely repent. The impenitent cannot have faith, because no promise has been made to them. On the contrary, they have been expressly assured that, as long as they remain impenitent, they have nothing to expect but eternal condemnation. Before a man can believe in Christ as his Savior, he must first see that he needs a Savior and must desire to have one. Only then can he or will he accept by faith the mercy which is offered to him in Christ.

Faith is Certainty.—Faith is the very opposite of doubt. True faith gives men the certainty of eternal life. For it is based on the promise of God. And "God is not a man that he should lie, nor the son of man that he should repent" (Num. 23:19). A Christian not only may but should be certain of his salvation. If he believes God's promise, how can he doubt it? His salvation is not at all dependent on what he may be able to do, but upon what Christ has done for Him, and on God's plain promise to give him everlasting life for Christ's sake. What Christ has done is complete and perfect, and what God has promised he will certainly perform.

Doubts.—Even true believers have seasons when their faith is tried and doubts assail them. Satan is ever active, seeking to cause them to fall from the faith. He endeavors to make them doubt God's grace and forgiveness and to lose their confidence in Him. But the Holy Spirit enables them to overcome. He dwells in their hearts and bears witness with their spirit that they are the children of God. When such periods of stress are over, the faith of the Christian grows all the stronger. He again has peace and unshaken confidence in Christ, and can say with St. Paul, "I know in whom I have believed" (2 Tim. 1:12).

Faith Should Grow.—Faith will save us, if it be a true faith, even though it be small or weak. But it ought to grow and increase in strength day by day like a healthy plant. We are to pray for its increase, and faithfully to use the means of grace. If we do, our faith will grow; and we shall be rooted and built up in Christ. As a result of such growth we shall have increasing confidence in God, greater joy and peace in our soul, deeper love to God and our fellow man, and greater strength to overcome the world.

Faith Should be Permanent.—Faith should not be spasmodic or occasional, but a firmly established and continuous condition of the soul. We are to trust in Christ and in the Triune God not only at times but always. Our whole life is to be one of faith. We are to permit nothing to separate us from the love of God in Christ Jesus, but to be faithful unto death, that we may receive the crown of everlasting life.

Faith May Decay and Die.—If it is fed and nourished on the Word of God, faith grows; but if not, it decays and dies. Some for a time believe, but in time of temptation fall away. Many make shipwreck of their faith by deliberately doing that which their own conscience tells them is wrong. Such shipwreck is sure to follow if Christ is not permitted to rule in the heart and the promptings of His Spirit are unheeded. When faith has perished, salvation is lost. It remains lost as long as such persons do not again come to true repentance and faith.

CHAPTER XVII. WE ARE SAVED BY FAITH ALONE WITHOUT WORKS

Those who enter into heaven will do so, not because they have deserved to enter, but because they believe in Christ their Savior. Salvation is altogether a gift of God's grace. It cannot be earned or merited by our works. We can only accept what God's grace offers through Christ. We are saved by faith alone without works.

Grace and Faith.—Salvation is spoken of in the Bible as becoming ours both by grace and by faith. But the same thing is meant by both terms. Salvation is by grace, because God bestows it upon us freely for Christ's sake and without any merit on our part. It is by faith, because by faith we accept the salvation which God freely offers. The relation between the two is expressed by St. Paul when he says, "By grace you are saved through faith" (Eph. 2:8).

Saved by Faith.—It is God's will that men should be saved by faith. When in His infinite love He sent His only Son into the world to redeem men, He did so in order that "whosoever believes on Him should not perish, but have everlasting life" (John 3:16). When the Savior had completed His work of redemption and sent His disciples forth to preach the Gospel to all nations, His words were, "He that believes and is baptized shall be saved; but he that does not believe shall be damned" (Mark 16:16). And when the Philippian jailor anxiously inquired what he must do to be saved, the answer of the apostle was, "Believe on the Lord Jesus Christ, and thou shalt be saved" (Acts 16:31).

Why Faith Saves.—Faith saves us, not because it is regarded by God as a merit on our part and therefore rewarded with salvation, but because it is the grateful acceptance of what God freely offers. It is no more a merit on our part than it is a merit on the part of the beggar when he reaches out his hand to receive the gift that is bestowed upon him.

We are Justified by Faith.—In order that we may be saved, we must first be pronounced by God to be righteous and fit to enter into heaven. This is expressed in the Bible by the word "justify." To be justified means to be pronounced righteous. We are justified by faith. For by faith we take hold of and cling to Christ and present Him before God as our substitute who has done for us all that needs to be done to make us righteous. If we believe in Him, then through Him we have met the strictest demands of God's justice; and when God looks on us, He beholds not our own guilt and unrighteousness, but the righteousness of Christ which we have put on by faith.

What Justification Is.—Justification is the sinner's acquittal from the charges of the law which he has broken. It is the act of God in which, as our Lawgiver and Judge, He pronounces us free for Christ's sake from the guilt of our sins and from the punishment which we have deserved. We are not by our justification made sinless and holy creatures. But by it the guilt of our sins is taken away, God's wrath and punishment are turned aside from us, and we are received into His favor. "Being justified by faith, we have peace with God through our Lord Jesus Christ" (Rom. 5:1).

Not by Works.—If men kept God's law perfectly, they would be saved by their works. But no man does or can keep it thus. We are born sinful beings, and break God's law daily in many ways. By our works we deserve not salvation but condemnation. So far as our works are concerned, we are under the curse; "for it is written. Cursed is every one that continues not in all the things that are written in the book of the law to do them" (Gal. 3:10).

It was because of men's unrighteousness and their utter inability to be anything else but unrighteous, that God sent His Son into the world to acquire righteousness for them. If they could have saved themselves, He would have let them do so, and would not have sent His only Son to suffer and die. But righteousness cannot come to us by keeping the law. The law simply shows us our sinfulness. It is meant to do so, and thus to become our school-master to bring us to Christ, in order that we may be justified by faith in Him.

By Faith Alone.—Our works have nothing to do with obtaining salvation, either before we believe or after we believe. Before we believe, we cannot do any good works; for whatever is not of faith is sin. And after we believe, we are already justified by our faith before we have any opportunity to do good works.

Everyone who has faith will do good works. But he will do them not in order to be saved,- but because he has faith and is saved. In our justification before God, nothing has any weight but the merits of Jesus Christ made ours by faith. If our works had anything to do with our justification, they would only cause us to be lost; for the works of even the best Christians are imperfect.

When St. James speaks of Abraham as being justified by his works, he refers to Abraham's works as the outward evidence of his justification; for two verses farther on he himself declares that Abraham believed God, and his faith was counted to him for righteousness.

In Old Testament Times.—Salvation by faith alone is not taught in the New Testament only, but in the Old Testament as well. Men have been justified and saved from the earliest times by faith and not by works. Men were just as sinful and helpless by nature then as now, and had to be saved by the same grace of God which saves us. Their faith was counted to them for righteousness, just as ours is. Abel, Enoch, Noah, Abraham, Isaac, Jacob, Joseph, Moses, Rahab and many others are described in the Scriptures as people who had faith and were on this account acceptable to God. The Savior had, indeed, not yet come. But they believed the promise of His coming, and had faith in the mercy of God.

It is true, God gave the Israelites His law and commanded them to obey it. But they were to keep it because they believed in Him as their God and loved Him and not for the purpose of earning salvation by their deeds. Faith is expressly mentioned as the condition of salvation. And we are told that God spared the Ninevites from the destruction which they had deserved by their sins, because they believed the preaching of His prophet Jonah. Although the doctrine of justification by faith is brought out more fully in the New Testament than in the Old, it is taught in the Old Testament also. God's way of salvation has been the same in every age. "The just shall live by faith" (Gal. 3:11). Men never were and never will be justified by works, but by faith alone.

CHAPTER XVIII. THE HOLY LIFE OF THE CHRISTIAN.

Although the Christian is not justified by his works but by faith alone, he will and must lead a holy life.

A New Creature.—The believer has been born again, "not of the will of the flesh nor of the will of man, but of God" (John 1:13). He is therefore "a new creature. Old things are passed away; all things are become new" (2 Cor. 5:17). His heart has been changed by grace. His mind is no longer at "enmity against God," but is conformed to God's mind. He now desires to do the very things which God wills that he should do. He has new aims and aspirations, new motives and principles of action, new desires and hopes. He is dead unto sin, but alive unto God. He lives, yet not he, but Christ lives in him; and the life which he now lives in the flesh he lives by faith in the Son of God, who loved him and gave Himself for him (Gal. 2:20).

A New Life.—Out of the heart are the issues of life. "As a man thinks in his heart, so he is" (Prov. 23:7). Since the believer's heart has been changed, his conduct is necessarily and inevitably changed also. His holy life is the outward evidence of the change that has taken place within him. He has been made a new creature in Christ Jesus that he might do good works, and was before ordained that he should walk in them. He therefore puts off "concerning the former conversation the old man which is corrupt according to the deceitful lusts," and becomes renewed in the spirit of his mind, and puts on "the new man which after God is created in righteousness and true holiness" (Eph. 2:22-24).

A Holy Life Necessary.—Those who are true believers do not and cannot live in sin. "How shall we who are dead to sin live any longer therein?" (Rom. 6:2). Faith is a new life principle in man and necessarily results in a new life of obedience to God. While our good works have nothing to do with our justification, faith that does not result in good works is dead. It is only a seeming and not a real faith. Living faith, like a good tree, will bear fruit. True believers are genuinely sorry for their sins, and they cannot, therefore, do otherwise than turn away from their sins and follow after holiness. The evil nature must be continually fought against and overcome. If it is not subdued and held in subjection, it will regain the mastery over him and cause him to fall from the faith.

Christ Demands It.—The Savior demands a holy life of His disciples. They are to let their light shine before men, that their good works may be seen and their Father in heaven glorified. If they love Him they are to keep commandments and follow His example. Not every one that says to Him, Lord, Lord, shall enter into the kingdom of heaven, but he that doeth the will of His Father who is in heaven. If men live after the flesh, they shall die; but if through the Spirit they mortify the deeds of the body, they shall live.

It Involves a Conflict.—To lead a holy life involves a constant inner conflict against sin. The frailty of human nature clings to the believer as long as he lives. "The spirit indeed is willing, but the flesh is weak" (Matt. 26:41). The old evil nature is not eradicated, but remains in him alongside of the new nature which God has given him. He delights in the law of God after the inward man; but there is a law in his members that wars against the law of his mind, and makes it difficult for him to do the will of God. "The flesh lusts against the spirit and the spirit against the flesh" (Gal. 5:17). The believer often finds with St. Paul, that the good which he would he does not, and the evil which he does.

None Perfectly Holy.—The Christian will never become perfectly holy in this world. The conflict of flesh and spirit will continue to the end of his life. He will never be entirely free from sins of weakness. He must live a life of daily repentance, that he may be daily forgiven. He will always have abundant occasion to pray each day in the words of the fifth petition of the Lord's Prayer, "Forgive us our trespasses, as we forgive those who trespass against us" (Matt. 6:12). For "if we say we have no sin, we deceive ourselves, and the truth is not in us. But if we confess our sins, God is faithful and just to forgive us our sins, and to cleanse us from all unrighteousness'' (1 John 1:8-9).

The Christian Aspires to be Holy.—Though the believer's attainments fall far short of his aim, he aspires to be perfect as his Father in heaven is perfect. Owing to the weakness which clings to us, we cannot keep God's law perfectly even with our best efforts. But we must try to do so. However lacking we may be in the perfection of our attainment, we must not be lacking in sincere and honest effort. Our aspirations and strivings are ever to be toward those things which are good and holy. "Whatsoever things are true, whatsoever are honest, whatsoever things are just, whatsoever things are pure, whatsoever things are lovely, whatsoever things are of good report, if there be any virtue, if there be any praise" (Phil. 4:8),—these are the things we are to think of and strive to attain. And when we fail to attain them, we are to be filled with genuine sorrow for our failure.

He Grows in Holiness.—When we are brought to faith in Christ and are thus born again, we are spiritual babes. But we are to grow till we reach the measure of the stature of the fullness of Christ. We shall reach His perfection only after we are transformed and glorified in the world to come. But we are to approach to it more and more even here on earth. We cannot do so by our own power; but we can by the help of God. His grace will support us. "He who has begun the good work in us will also perform it" (Phil. 1:6), to the end He sanctifies us through the truth; His word is truth. The Gospel, when received by faith, becomes a power in our hearts and lives to conform us more and more to a likeness with Jesus our Savior.

What We Must Do.—But in order that this end may be attained, we ourselves must cooperate with the grace of God. We must diligently hear and read God's Word, heed its reproof, obey its commands, and accept its consolations. We must obey the promptings of the Holy Spirit within us, and never deliberately do what is wrong. We must watch and pray that we enter not into temptation. And we must constantly seek help and strength from God to overcome the sinful promptings of our own heart, the allurements of the world, and the whisperings of Satan.

His Motives.—The holiness of the Christian is not a matter to be settled between him and the law of Moses. Believing in Christ, he has through Christ fulfilled that law and is free from it. It is not the old law of Moses that constrains the Christian to lead a new life, but the new law of the Gospel, a law operating, not from without, but from within. It is a law which says, not like that of Moses, "Do this or omit that under penalty of punishment," but which says "the love of Christ constrains me" (1 Cor. 5:15). It is not the fear of punishment, but the love of God implanted in the heart, which actuates the believer to lead a life of holiness. As his faith grows stronger and his love to God deepens, his life becomes more and more conformed to God's will.

The Law not Abrogated.—While Christ has freed the Christian from the Mosaic law, He has not annulled that law nor its decree against sin. It is only he who has true faith and who therefore has truly repented of sin, who is freed from the alternative of fulfilling that law or else suffering its penalty. All others are still bound by it. The wages of sin still is death. Sin unrepented of leads to eternal destruction. For this reason the believer dare not argue that because he has fulfilled the law in Christ and is free from it, he may sin with impunity. If he sins wilfully, he lacks repentance and therefore lacks faith. Such a person is still under the law and subject to its condemnation. Those who make the grace of God a cloak for an impenitent persistence in sin will find themselves on the Day of Judgment placed in the same class with those who never professed to believe in Christ, and will share eternal punishment with them.

CHAPTER XIX. CONCERNING SATAN THE TEMPTER.

The Christian must not only contend against the promptings of his own evil nature within him, but against the temptations of Satan.

Who Satan Is.—Satan is not an evil principle in man tempting him to sin. For the Savior had no evil principle in Him, yet He was tempted forty days and forty nights by the devil. Satan is a person, a wicked spirit. He was not created evil, but was once a good angel; for everything that God made was good. But he sinned against God and became a bad angel, a devil. The Bible does not expressly state what the sin was which he committed; but it probably was pride or a desire to be equal with God.

How Described.—Satan is described in the Bible as the originator of sin, a liar and murderer from the beginning. He is the serpent who beguiled Eve by his subtilty, who deceives the whole world, and who seeks to corrupt the minds of the Christians. He is the one whose power, Jesus came into the world to break, and who otherwise would have continued to hold us in bondage and oppression. He is the wicked spirit who works in the children of disobedience. He is the god of this world whom the wicked serve, and who keeps them in his service by blinding their minds so that the light of the Gospel does not shine into them. He is an exceedingly powerful foe, to prevail against whom Christians must put on the whole armor of God, that they may be able to withstand in the evil hour, and, having done all, to stand" (Eph. 6:11-13).

His Names.—The name Satan means adversary, and he is so called because he is the bitter foe of God and man. He is called the devil, or accuser, because he accuses men before God and demands of God's justice that the same punishment which is measured out to him for his sins be inflicted on men for their sins. He is called Belial, the worthless one. He is called also the prince of this world, because he rules in the hearts of impenitent men; and the god of this world, because he is the master whom they worship and serve by their sin. He is the great Dragon or serpent whose power and subtlety are to be dreaded and guarded against.

A Chief.—Satan is not the only fallen angel. Though he is frequently called the devil by pre-eminence, there are many devils. There was a whole legion of them in the demoniac of Gadara. When Satan fell, he carried many other angels with him, having persuaded them also to sin against God. There is a kingdom of darkness and evil not only in a figurative but an actual sense,—a kingdom in which there are various ranks, principalities, powers and rulers. Satan is its chief, the prince of darkness, who has under him innumerable other spirits. While these wicked spirits are at war with God and pious men, they are at one among themselves; if they were not, their kingdom

His Power.—Satan and his angels by their fall lost the heavenly glory which had been theirs. But just as man retained much of his power after the fall, so the wicked angels retained much of theirs. They still remain powerful spirits, though now their powers are directed solely toward that which is evil. They hate God, and are filled with envy and rage against the good angels and pious men. Their power is exceedingly great,—far greater than that of man. But it is limited by God. They can do no more than God permits them to do. They are already suffering some of the penalties of their sin. They are banished from the presence of God, cast down into hell, and given over to their own evil thoughts and ways. But a greater punishment still is reserved for them. On the Day of Judgment they shall be cast into the lake of fire and brimstone, to be tormented day and night forever.

His Aim.—Satan cannot harm God; therefore he tries to harm men, whom God loves. He brings all his resources to bear upon them to lead them to destruction. He goes about as a roaring lion seeking whom he may devour (1 Pet. 5:8). He endeavors to harm them in body and property as well as in soul. It was he who brought the terrible succession of calamities upon Job, and who constantly tormented St. Paul with a physical affliction. In the Savior's time he frequently took possession of men's bodies. But his chief aim is to ruin men's souls and thus frustrate God's gracious purpose of saving them.

He Seeks to Prevent Men from Believing.—Satan endeavors to harden men in their sins, so that they may not obey the truth of the Gospel. For this purpose he makes the world with its business and pleasures as attractive to them as possible, and tempts them to those sins to which their own natural heart most strongly inclines them. And when they hear the Word of God, he immediately comes and takes it out of their hearts, lest they should believe and be saved.

He Seeks to Destroy the Believers.—Satan not only tries to prevent men from believing, but does his utmost to win back those who do believe. He tempts them to sin and unbelief. And unless they are constantly on their guard against him, he will lead them to destruction.

He is the Tempter.—It was Satan who persuaded Eve to doubt God's word and transgress His command. And he has been behind every sin that has been committed since that time. It was he who tempted Peter to deny his Lord; who put it into the heart of Judas Iscariot to betray the Savior; and who filled the heart of Ananias to lie to the Holy Ghost and keep back part of the price of his land. It is he who tempts all men and leads them on in the way of sin.

How He Comes.—Satan seldom reveals his real purpose when he tempts men. He does not give warning of his approach, but is exceedingly subtle and cunning. The statement that he goes about as a roaring lion is meant to give expression to his power and his thirst for men's souls, but does not describe the manner of his approach. He transforms himself into an angel of light. He poses as our friend and well-wisher. He pretended that he was pointing out to Eve how to attain greater happiness, and that he did not like to see the Savior suffer hunger. He represents the course of sin which he desires us to follow as the very course which will bring us most happiness. He minimizes its sinfulness and danger, tells us we are not expected to deny ourselves all pleasure in life, and points to the example of others who do as he desires us to do. He tempts us through the desires of our own heart, through the objects of sense around us, through wicked men, and sometimes even through those who really mean to be our friends but who are themselves deceived by Satan.

He Must Be Resisted.—If we resist the devil, he will flee from us. But if we yield to him, he will come to us more and more with his evil promptings and finally bring us completely under his dominion. We must not underrate his power; for he is the head of a powerful kingdom of evil. In contending against him "we wrestle not against flesh and blood, but against principalities, against powers, against the rulers of the darkness of this world, against spiritual wickedness in high places" (Eph. 6:12). To fight against him means vastly more than to contend against men. We could not possibly win by our own power. But every believer can win the victory with God's help.

The Means to be Used.—The means which we must use in order to overcome the devil are watchfulness, the Word of God, faith, and prayer. With these weapons Christ was victorious over Satan in the wilderness, and with these we also can conquer. If we fail to do so, it will be our own fault, because we do not use the means which God places at our disposal. Powerful as the devil is, he cannot harm those who sincerely live by faith in Christ. The Savior has delivered us from the power of the devil. He gives us power to overcome Satan's temptations; and He shields us against Satan's accusations by holding up His own sufferings as a complete satisfaction to God's justice for our sins.

CHAPTER XX.
THE CHRISTIAN CHURCH.

On the day of Pentecost, ten days after His ascension into heaven, Christ poured out the Holy Spirit upon the apostles and thus founded His Church. For it was after the outpouring of the Holy Ghost that the Gospel of the crucified and risen Savior was first preached, that the first converts were made, and the first Christian baptisms performed.

What the Church Is.—The Church is "the communion of saints" or, in other words, the fellowship of those who are true believers in Christ. It is the institution through which the Holy Spirit carries on His saving work of applying the redemption of Christ to the souls of men through the Word of God and the sacraments; and in which He gathers, guides and sanctifies those whom He has brought to faith. The Church is found wherever the Gospel is preached in its purity and the sacraments are rightly administered. For wherever these are found, there are also found some who truly believe.

Invisible.—As a spiritual fellowship of believers, the Church is invisible. The bodies of believers can of course be seen, and their faith can be recognized by their works. But as one man cannot read the heart of another, no one can tell just who is a believer and who is not. God alone can tell who are His. Christ knows His own.

In What Sense Visible.—The Church may also be regarded as an external organization. In this sense the Church is visible, and includes all those who are outwardly united with those who profess to be

Christians. It is composed of many individual churches scattered throughout the world and belonging to many different denominations, who with more or less purity teach the doctrine of salvation through faith in Christ. It includes many who are not really believers at heart, and whom Christ, therefore, does not recognize as member of the true and invisible Church. There are tares among the wheat; and because of the outward similarity between them, they cannot be told apart or separated by man. They will remain side by side until the judgment day, when they will be separated from one another by the angels.

On Earth and in Heaven.—The Church, being identical with the Kingdom of God, is found both on earth and in heaven. To the Church in heaven belong those who have died in the faith and have gone to their eternal reward. It is called the Church Triumphant, because its members have won the victory of faith and through the power of Christ have triumphed over all their foes. The Church on earth is called the Church Militant; that is, the Church which is still fighting the good fight of faith. None will ever belong to the Church Triumphant who have not belonged to the Church Militant. Unless men are believers they cannot be saved. He who does not fight the battle cannot win the victory. All those in the Church Militant who are faithful unto death shall belong to the Church Triumphant. Him that overcomes, Christ will grant to sit with Him in His throne, even as He overcame and is set down with His Father in His throne.

But One Church.—The Christians are divided into many different churches, denominations and sects. But the Church itself is essentially one. It is composed of the true believers out of all these churches and denominations. There is one flock and one shepherd. Believers may and do live in widely separated places, and are distinguished by many differences of race, language and custom. But as members of the Church they are one. It is for this reason that the Church is called the Catholic (not Roman Catholic) or Universal Church.

Other Names.—The Church is called Holy, because the Holy Spirit is constantly at work in it, seeking to make men holy; and because its members, while by no means perfect, lead holy lives by the grace of God. It is called the Christian Church, because it is composed of those who believe in Christ. It is called Apostolic, because its faith rests on the witness and preaching of the apostles, who were with Christ, heard what He said, and saw what He did and suffered.

Christ and the Church.—The Church is the body of Christ, and He is its head. He is the Lord of the Church. He rules in it by grace; and He defends it against its enemies, so that the gates of hell shall not prevail against it.

Believers United with Christ.—The members of the Church are intimately united with Christ. He is the Head; they are the body. He is the vine; they are the branches. They can live spiritually only when they abide in Him by faith. Every branch that does not bear fruit is cut off and cast away. Such a person ceases to be a member of Christ's Church, though he may outwardly continue his connection with the visible Church.

United with One Another.—Being members of the one body of Christ, believers are not only united to Christ by faith, but through Him are united to one another. They are, therefore, to dwell together in love, and keep the unity of the Spirit in the bond of peace. Each believer has his own particular work and functions to perform as a member of Christ's body. Each is useful and necessary in his place, even the humblest. One cannot say to the other that he has no need of him, just as the eye cannot say to the hand or the head to the feet, "I have no need of you" (1 Cor. 12:21). All the members of the Church are to work together in harmony for the accomplishment of the ends which Christ their Head desires.

Its Work.—Christ has given His Church a work to do. It is to make disciples of all nations. The apostles to whom the command was given to go forth into all the world and preach the Gospel to every creature were the representatives of the whole Church, and through them the work was laid on all. The Church is the human instrumentality through which the Holy Spirit carries on His work in the souls of men.

Its Tools.—In order to do its work, the Church has been supplied with appropriate tools. These are the Word of God and the two sacraments, Baptism and the Lord's Supper. They are the means of grace. The Church is to preach the Word and administer the sacraments, in order that through them men may obtain the blessings of Christ's redemption. These tools are mighty for the accomplishment of the Church's work, because they are endowed with supernatural power by the Holy Spirit. They are the power of God unto salvation, not because those who handle them to possess such extraordinary skill in their use, but because the Holy Spirit works through them. It is the Holy Spirit who regenerates, converts, renews and sanctifies men.

Its Workmen.—The actual preaching of the Word and the administration of the sacraments, as well as the exercise of the power to declare the remission of sins to believers, is committed to those who are set apart to the Christian ministry. They are to be properly called and ordained to the office by the Church. They are not the successors of the apostles; for while the apostles also exercised all the functions of the Christian ministry, they held a much higher position than the ministry. The apostles were the witnesses of all that

Christ did and suffered; and on their testimony, as given in their preaching and writings, the Church rests.

Their Rank.—The New Testament recognizes no differences of rank in the ministry. Presbyters or elders and bishops or overseers were but different names for the same office and were used interchangeably. It was only at a later period that the office of a bishop was made superior to that of the regular ministry.

Their Duties.—Ministers are ambassadors of Christ to beseech men to be reconciled to God. God speaks to men through them. He who hears them, hears Christ; he who despises them, despises Christ. They are to preach the Word in season and out of season, whether men will heed or not. They are to watch over the flock over which the Holy Ghost has made them overseers. They are answerable for the souls committed to their charge: and they are to be obeyed as those who have the rule over us. They are to set a good example of holy living. Should any of them be hypocrites, however, their hypocrisy would not invalidate their official acts. The unbelief of man cannot make the promise of God of none effect.

CHAPTER XXI. THE BIBLE IS THE WORD OF GOD.

The first and most important of the Church's tools for doing its work is the Bible.

Why the Bible is Needed.—Nature tells of the existence of God, but does not reveal His will. Conscience tells us something of His will, but its knowledge has become very dim since the Fall into sin. Neither nature nor conscience can tell us anything of God's gracious plan of salvation in Jesus Christ. Therefore, if we are to have any adequate knowledge of God's will, and any knowledge at all of His infinite love and grace, it must be through a special revelation of God. This revelation has been given to us in the Bible.

What the Bible Contains.—The Bible consists of the Old and New Testaments. It contains Law and Gospel,—Law, telling us what we ought to do, and Gospel, telling us how we are to be saved. It contains narratives and prophecies also, which are not strictly a part of either Law or Gospel, but which may be arranged under one or the other head as having a direct or indirect relation to it. The Old Testament is often spoken of as containing the Law, and the New Testament as containing the Gospel. Strictly speaking, there is Law and Gospel in both; but the Law predominates in the Old, and the Gospel in the New Testament. The Gospel of the Old Testament is prophetical; in the New Testament it is based on an accomplished fact. The Old Testament was preparatory to the New; and the New Testament is the fulfilment of the Old. The New Testament is the culmination of God's revelation to man.

The Bible God's Word.—The Bible is the Word of God. It is not a book of human devising, but was written "by the inspiration of God" (2 Tim. 3:16). It not only contains God's Word, but it is His Word. It is an inspired Book.

The Old Testament.—We have the testimony of the Lord Jesus Christ Himself for the divine authority of the Old Testament. He quoted from it as an infallible source of appeal when He repelled the temptations of Satan in the wilderness. At other times also He referred to its divine authority. Throughout the entire New Testament the inspiration of the Old Testament is taken as an established fact. Peter and Paul give explicit expression to this fact when they tell us that "the prophecy came not, of old time by the will of man, but holy men of God spoke as they were moved by the Holy Ghost" (2 Pet. 1:21) and that "all Scripture is given by inspiration of God" (2 Tim. 3:16).

The New Testament.—Christ promised His disciples that He would send them the Holy Spirit to guide them into all truth. This promise was fulfilled on Pentecost when the Holy Ghost was poured out upon the disciples. They at once began to preach the Gospel. And ever afterwards they were conscious of speaking by inspiration of the Holy Ghost, and consequently of speaking that which was infallibly true. If even an angel from heaven taught anything different from that which they taught, he should be accursed.

What the apostles wrote was identical in substance with what they preached. It was the same Gospel and was uttered by inspiration of the same Spirit. Therefore St. Paul commanded the Thessalonians to hold fast all that they had learned from him, whether by word of mouth or by letter. He commanded them to read his epistle to all the brethren, and thereby intimated that they were to pay as much heed to it as they would to the same truths if uttered by him in person. He does, indeed, at one place distinguish between what he says and what Christ says; but he asserts in the very same chapter also, that He has the Spirit of the Lord. He expressly declares that what he is writing are the commands of the Lord. And he thanks God that the Thessalonians received his utterances, not as the word of man, but as they were in truth, the Word of God.

Peculiarities of Style.—The style in which the various books of the Bible are written bear traces of the characteristics of their several authors. The apostles have left the impress of their personality upon their writings. This is especially the case with St. John and St. Paul. But this does not argue against the inspiration of what they wrote. They did not write as mere machines. God used them and their diversified talents for the purpose of conveying His will to men. The Holy Spirit put into their minds and hearts what to write, and directed them in the writing itself, so that they did not err in any matter that affected His will. But He did not destroy their individuality. Each wrote in the style peculiar to himself. Sometimes they even added matters of a strictly personal nature, such as Paul's request to Timothy to bring his cloak to him, and the personal advice which he gives Timothy concerning his health.

How They Wrote.—The writers of the Biblical books wrote as men to men, and often strained every faculty of their mind to the utmost, as is evident from the impassioned utterances, elaborate arguments and sudden transitions in St. Paul's epistles. But at the same time they wrote as they were moved by the Holy Ghost, and produced a correct and unerring record of everything that the Holy Ghost desired to communicate to men, and of all that in any way affects the truth of salvation.

The Gospel Records.—The contrast which may be found between the Gospels of Matthew, Mark and Luke on the one hand and that of John on the other is due to their different way of treating the history of our Lord. The first three evangelists start with the human nature of Christ and lead us up to His divinity, while John starts with the divine nature, the eternal Word, and leads us down to the humanity of Christ. Both narratives give the same history, but from u different standpoint. By taking them together we have a complete view of the God-man, both from the human and the divine side of His Being.

The Bible and Science.—As the Bible does not undertake to teach science but religion, it is to be regarded from the religious and not the scientific standpoint. It is not to be expected to teach the results of human investigation. Its writers were inspired by the Holy Spirit with a supernatural knowledge of religion; but on other subjects they knew no more than the other men of their day. Yet when the facts of science are well established and are not mere theories, they are found to harmonize in a remarkable manner with the Holy Scriptures. The more the secrets of nature and of history are brought to light, the more corroboration they give to the teachings and narratives of the Bible.

The Bible Its Own Best Witness.—The inspiration of the Bible is proved by its contents. It contains information which no man by his own power could ever have discovered or known. It foretells events which no uninspired man could ever have foreseen. It contains teachings so exalted, that they could never have originated in the depraved heart of man, and are not even approached by the writings of the noblest among the heathen sages and philosophers. It gives evidence of a divine power such as no book of simply human origin ever did or can possess. Its power is manifest in all the history of the Church's past, and in the Church today. Every conversion is a miracle of God's grace, wrought through the Word of God. We cannot hear or read the Bible without feeling and knowing by the manner in which it takes hold on our heart, that God Himself is speaking to us and searching out the innermost recesses of our soul. For "the Word of God is quick and powerful, and sharper than any two-edged sword, piercing even to the dividing asunder of soul and spirit and of the joints and marrow, and is a discerner of the thoughts and intents of the heart" (Heb. 4:12).

Why It was Written.—The Bible was "written for our learning, that we through patience and comfort of the Scriptures might have hope" (Rom. 15:4). It is meant to be a lamp unto our feet and a light unto our path, to lead us through the darkness of this world to our home in heaven. It contains all that we need to know of God in this world, and all that is necessary to lead us to repentance, to faith, and to a right Christian life. Its center and core is Christ, in whom lies our only but sure hope of salvation. It is an unerring guide to the truth. It is the final and absolute authority in matters of religion. Before it, all human authority, however great, must bow and give way. Anyone who teaches contrary to it is accursed. Anyone who adds to or subtracts from its teachings shall be stricken from God's book of life. It is the only revelation which God will give to all men. If its testimony is not accepted, God will not send any one back from the dead to assure men of its truth. We must take heed, therefore, to what it says. If we fail to do so, we shall be lost.

CHAPTER XXII.
BAPTISM.

When Jesus was about to ascend into heaven, He commanded His disciples to go into all the world and make disciples of all nations, baptizing them in the name of the Father and of the Son and of the Holy Ghost, and teaching them to observe all things whatsoever He had commanded (Matt. 28:19). Those who believe and are baptized shall be saved, but those who do not believe shall be damned.

What Baptism Is.—Baptism consists in applying water to a person "in the name of the Father and of the Son and of the Holy Ghost" (Matt. 28:19) in accordance with Christ's command. A distinction must be made between the baptism administered by the disciples after Christ's ascension and that administered by John the Baptist. That of John was a baptism unto repentance. It was only an outward sign or symbol of the spiritual cleansing which had taken place in men through their repentance. It did not confer any particular grace of God. But Christian baptism is a means of grace—a channel through which the Holy Spirit confers special blessings upon us. It is the means through which He produces regeneration or the new birth in the hearts of children, and the means through which He formally introduces adults into the kingdom of God as His disciples, after they have been regenerated or brought to faith through the Word of God.

What Baptism Does.—Those who are baptized are received into the covenant with God, and become sharers in the atoning death of Jesus. They are baptized into Christ's death; and all that He has done is thrown open them and becomes their possession, if they believe. To the believer, therefore, baptism brings the forgiveness of sins and everlasting life. It is a washing away of sin, and a washing of regeneration by the Holy Ghost. It is God's way of adopting us as His children, and making us heirs of everlasting life.

Why Necessary.—Baptism is necessary for all, because Christ has commanded all to be baptized, and because He has connected the blessings of salvation with it. Those who neglect or despise baptism are, therefore, disobedient to Christ, and deprive themselves of the blessings which He has connected with this sacrament. Just as Naaman, the Syrian, could not have been cured of his leprosy, if he had refused to go to the Jordan and wash when the prophet told him to go; so men cannot be cured of the leprosy of their sin, if they refuse to be baptized. It was not the water of the Jordan that cured Naaman; and yet without that water he could not have been cured, because the promise was bound up with the use of the water and would not have availed him otherwise. It is not the water in baptism that cures us of our sins; yet without the water we cannot be cured, because the promise of forgiveness and salvation is bound up with the water of baptism. It is the promise of God that gives baptism its value, and our faith which makes its blessings our own.

The Mode of Baptism.—Baptism may be administered either by immersion of the whole body in water, or by pouring or sprinkling water on the head. Baptism administered by immersion is valid baptism; but it is not advisable, especially in our climate. Immersion is not essential. Baptism is just as valid if performed by the more convenient mode of pouring or sprinkling; and it is thus administered by the majority of Christian churches. It is not the amount of water, but the application of water in the name of the Father and of the Son and of the Holy Ghost that makes baptism what it is. In many cases, such as extreme sickness, it would be impossible to administer baptism, however greatly desired by the patient, if it had to be done by immersion. And yet Christ has commanded all men to be baptized, and certainly wants none to be excluded who sincerely desire to receive baptism.

Meaning of the Word.—The Savior did not coin a new word to designate this sacrament. He employed a Greek word which was already in use. That word, from which our English word "baptize" is derived, does not necessarily mean to immerse, but to apply water or to wash. It is so used in the Gospel of St. Mark where it says that the Pharisees, when they came from market, would not eat unless they washed (Greek baptized). In his letter to the Corinthians, St. Paul uses the same word in the sense of sprinkling, when he refers to the sprinkling of spray upon the Israelites while they passed through the Red Sea under the guidance of Moses.

How the Apostles Baptized.—In the case of the Philippian jailor and the three thousand persons who were baptized on the day of Pentecost, baptism by immersion was extremely unlikely if not impossible, on account of the scarcity of water for such a purpose. The jailor was baptized in the prison; and the three thousand were baptized in Jerusalem, with no stream of any depth nearer than the Jordan, miles away. Though we are not informed by the Bible what mode of baptism was pursued in these cases, it is hard to see how any other but that of pouring or sprinkling could have been employed.

How Jesus was Baptized.—We are not told whether Jesus was immersed in the Jordan, or whether John baptized Him by pouring water on His head. We are told that Jesus came up out of the water after He was baptized. But He would have done that, just as much if He stood in the stream while John poured water on His head, as He would if He had been immersed.

Children to be Baptized.—Children are to be baptized. They constitute a large and important part of the "nations" whom Christ commanded His disciples to baptize. The kingdom of God is composed of little children and of those who become as little children. They have a right, therefore to receive that sacrament by which we enter into the kingdom of God. Christ expressly commands that children be brought to Him; and there is no more effective way of bringing them to Him, than that which He Himself has pointed out in His command to baptize and teach all men. In Old Testament times children at the age of eight were received by the rite of circumcision into the covenant made by God with Abraham; and it is unreasonable to suppose that they should be excluded from the New Testament covenant, which is entered by baptism. Peter assured the Jews, "The promise is unto you and to your children." And when men believed the preaching of the Gospel, the apostles baptized them and their household.

Children Need Baptism.—Though not yet guilty of conscious and actual transgressions, infants are by nature sinful. The germs of sin are in them. And if the children live to grow up, those germs will develop into sinful deeds. Children often die in infancy; and death is the result of sin. If, therefore, they are to enter the kingdom of God, they also must be born again. It is doubtless that the Holy Spirit can implant a new spiritual life in children without the use of external means. But since baptism is a washing of regeneration, we have no right to deprive them of that sacrament which is the ordinary way in which the Holy Spirit produces the new birth within them.

Faith Necessary.—Not all who are baptized will be saved, but only those who believe and are baptized. Those who do not believe are lost. God receives us into

His covenant and adopts us as His children in Holy Baptism. But, as disobedient and rebellious children are disinherited by earthly parents, so our heavenly Father disinherits those baptized persons who live in impenitence and unbelief. They lose that eternal and glorious inheritance which would have been theirs, if they had remained faithful.

Baptism Permanent.—Baptism once properly administered is not to be repeated. It is permanent. It is a covenant between God and man. Though man is often unfaithful to his part of the covenant, God never is. His promises are all yes and Amen. The unbelief of men does not make the promise of God of none effect. Baptized persons who are lost perish, not because of any change in God, but because of the change in themselves. God's covenant stands. All who comply with its conditions receive its benefits; those who do not, lose them. Yet, if these latter come back to God in true repentance, they are received by God and re-instated in their baptismal privileges. They need not be baptized again; the old baptism stands. The rebellious son who repents and is forgiven needs not to be adopted again as a son. His reception and forgiveness by his father are all that are necessary to reinstate him in the privileges of sonship.

Confirmation.—The rite of confirmation is intimately associated with the baptism of children. When those who were baptized in infancy have arrived at an age at which they are able to examine themselves, they are to be confirmed. After receiving from the pastor the further instruction which they need, they make a public confession of the faith in which they were baptized—a confession involving not merely a recitation of the Creed believed in by the Church, but a declaration of trust in God and His Word such as is taught in the explanation of the Creed in the Catechism. The minister then lays his hand on the head of each, while he and the congregation pray that God may give His Holy Spirit to each severally to keep him in the true faith and to make him grow in holiness. Those who are thus confirmed are admitted to the Lord's Supper. They were already members of the Church by virtue of their baptism; but having been confirmed, they become communicant members.

While there is no command in the Scriptures for the rite of confirmation, it is a useful ordinance of the Church and is in strict harmony with the spirit of the Bible. Christ has commanded that those who are baptized shall be taught all things whatsoever He has commanded; and He has said that those who want Him to confess them before His heavenly Father must confess Him before men. Confirmation is in line with both these commands of Christ; for it is preceded by a thorough instruction in the teachings of Christ, and involves a public confession of His name.

CHAPTER XXIII.
THE LORD'S SUPPER.

"The Lord Jesus Christ, the same night in which he was betrayed, took bread; and when He had given thanks, He brake it and gave it to His disciples, saying, Take, eat; this is my body which is given for you. This do in remembrance of me.

"After the same manner also He took the cup, when He had supped, gave thanks, and gave it to them saying, Drink ye all of it; this cup is the New Testament in my blood which is shed for you and for many for the remission of sins. This do ye, as oft as ye drink it, in remembrance of me" (1 Cor. 11:23-24). Thus our Savior instituted the Lord's Supper, or the Sacrament of the Altar.

What the Lord's Supper Is.—In, with and under the bread and wine which are used in the Lord's Supper, Christ gives the communicant His body and blood. For He says, "Take, eat, this is my body which is given for you," and "Drink all of it; this is my blood of the New Testament, which is shed for many for the remission of sins" (Matt. 26:28).

The Earthly Elements.—Bread and wine are used in the Lord's Supper because these are the earthly elements which Christ used when He instituted this sacrament. It is unlawful to substitute anything else in the place of either. The wafer so frequently used in Lutheran churches is unleavened bread. The Lord Himself used that kind; for He instituted the Lord's Supper at the time of the Jewish Passover, when the

Jews were forbidden to eat any other than unleavened bread.

What is Given Through Them.—Bread and wine are not all that is given in the Lord's Supper. They are not mere symbols of spiritual things; nor are they to be partaken of simply in order to bring Christ to our remembrance, though this is one purpose of the sacrament. The bread does not simply represent the body of Christ, nor the wine simply represent the blood of Christ. But they are the earthly elements through which in some way, mysterious yet real, the true body and blood of Christ are received by the communicant.

There is no transubstantiation; that is, the bread is not turned into the body of Christ, nor the wine into the blood of Christ. The bread and wine remain real bread and wine throughout the administration of the sacrament. Their substance remains unchanged. But there is a communion of the bread and wine with the body and blood of Christ, that when the communicant receives the former he receives the latter also. This communion is not a consubstantiation or combination of the bread and wine with the body and blood of Christ in such a manner as to form a third substance different from both. But the bread and wine become the vehicles through which the heavenly gift of Christ's body and blood, which were given and shed for us for the remission of sins, are communicated to us. It is this that makes the Lord's Supper a means of grace.

A Mystery.—The Lord's Supper is indeed a great mystery, just as many other teachings of the Bible are mysteries to us. But it is the part of faith to accept the teaching of Christ and His word, even when, like Nicodemus, we do not understand how such things can be. We must not, like some of Christ's disciples, turn from Him, because some of His teachings are beyond our human comprehension.

Its Object.—The object of the Lord's Supper is to give us the firm assurance of the forgiveness of our sins, thus to comfort our souls and strengthen our faith. It does this, because the body and blood of Christ received in the sacrament are the "body which was given for us and the blood which was shed for us for the remission of sins." If they are received in faith, they confer upon the communicant all the blessings which Christ secured by His sufferings and death. This sacrament is of special comfort, because each individually receives the bread and wine, and thus each individually receives also the assurance that the body of Christ was given and the blood of Christ shed for him.

How to be Received.—Those who come to the Lord's Supper must examine themselves beforehand, and prepare themselves to partake of it worthily. Both the believing and the unbelieving communicants receive the body and blood of Christ. But the unbelieving receive only a curse from it; for "he that eats and drinks unworthily, eats and drinks damnation to himself, not discerning the Lord's body" (1 Cor. 11:29). Just as men fail to receive a blessing, and receive instead only a deeper condemnation, if they do not believe the Word of God in which Christ comes to them; so they receive all the deeper condemnation also, if they do not believingly receive Christ when He comes to them in the Lord's Supper. Only he who comes to the Lord's Supper with penitent and believing heart, mourning over his sins, desiring forgiveness, and trusting in the grace of God in Christ, receives the blessings which the Savior desires to bestow.

Its Names.—This sacrament is called the Lord's Supper, because it was instituted by the Lord, and was first held at a time when the apostles were eating their supper. It is called the Sacrament of the Altar, because from the earliest times it was celebrated at the altar. It is called the Table of the Lord, because the Lord here gives us food and drink for our souls. It is called the Communion, because it is a communion of the bread and wine with the body and blood of Christ, a communion of believers with Christ, and a communion of believers with one another. It is sometimes called also the Eucharist, a name derived from a Greek word meaning to give thanks, because the administration of the sacrament is attended with thanksgiving.

The Confessional Service.—The administration of the Lord's Supper is preceded by a service of confession and absolution. This service is held, in order that those who desire to come to the Lord's Table may be prepared to come worthily. At this service they make public confession of their sins, of their faith in Christ, and of their determination by the grace of God to lead a holy life. And the minister, using the Power of the Keys conferred by Christ upon the Church when He says, "Whosesoever sins you forgive, they are forgiven unto them, and whosesoever sins you retain, they are retained" (John 20:23), pronounces the absolution upon them, In the name of the Father, and of the Son and of the Holy Ghost, he declares the forgiveness of their sins to all those who truly repent and believe in Christ, and the retention of their sins to all those who are impenitent and unbelieving.

CHAPTER XXIV. DEATH OF THE BODY AND ITS RESURRECTION ON THE LAST DAY.

Excepting those who shall be alive at the second coming of Christ, all men must die. The body shall return to the earth from which it was taken, and the soul shall go forth into eternity. But on the last day the body shall be raised to life again and reunited with the soul forever.

Why Men Die.—If men were not sinful, they would not have to die; their bodies as well as their souls would be immortal. But when sin entered the world, death entered with it. Death is the penalty of sin. And it comes upon all, because all are guilty. "As by one man sin entered into the world and death by sin; so death passed upon all men, because all men have sinned" (Rom. 5:12). For this reason "it is appointed unto men once to die" (Heb. 9:27).

How and When.—No one knows how long he will live. No one can tell at what moment or in what manner he will die. He may be called away while he is young, or be permitted to spend many years on earth. He may die suddenly, or receive long previous warning of the approaching end He may die through accident or disease. Die he surely will, but God alone knows when and how. We ought therefore to live in constant repentance and faith, that death may not come to us and find us unprepared to appear before God.

Our Days Numbered.—Man's days on earth are numbered. There is a limit set, beyond which he cannot pass. When that number is complete, he must die. All his efforts and those of his fellow-men cannot make him live a minute longer. But while men cannot live beyond their allotted time, they may and often do shorten their life. Through failure to take proper care of their body, by breaking the laws of health, and by a course of wickedness and dissipation, many people scarcely live out half their days.

The Terrors of Death.—Men shrink from death and avoid it as long as possible. For impenitent persons it is an object of unalloyed dread. It puts an end to all their hopes and joys. They live only for this world, and therefore death robs them of all that is dear to them. It sends them forth into eternity unprepared, and doomed to everlasting woe and despair.

Its Terrors Lost for the Christian.—For the believer death has lost its terrors. Even the Christian may shrink from death through the weakness of the flesh. Death is an unnatural thing. It was not meant by God to come upon men. It came as the result and penalty of sin. But, the believer does not fear death as the unbeliever does. Christ has robbed death of its sting and the grave of its victory. He has brought life and immortality to light. Death is in reality the Christian's friend, because it is the portal through which he escapes from a world of sin and sorrow and enters upon his eternal inheritance in heaven. For this reason the death of believers is spoken of in terms that lack all ideas of terror. They are gathered to their people, they are taken away from the evil to come, they fall asleep in with Christ.

Why Believers Also Must Die.—Christ has delivered the Christians from spiritual and eternal death, but not from bodily death. Their bodies are mortal as well as those of the unbelievers. Death in their case is, however, no longer to be regarded as a punishment for their sins. Christ has taken away all their punishment. But, their body must undergo a complete change before it can be fi; to enter heaven. It is an earthly, sinful body. It must be made a spiritual body. Flesh and blood cannot inherit the kingdom of God; neither doth corruption inherit incorruption. The body must die and decay, in order that it may be raised from the dead transformed and glorified. Just as the soul must be changed by the new birth before it can be fitted for entrance into heaven, so a similar change must take place in the body. The soul, having been born again in this world, enters upon its rest at once after death. But, the body must die and decay in the earth in order that from it as a seed or germ God may raise up at the last day an incorruptible, sinless, perfect and glorious body. This is the reason why those who are alive at Christ's second coming shall be changed. They shall not die; but the same change which has taken place in the others through death and the resurrection shall take place in them in a moment, in the twinkling of an eye, at the last trumpet.

The Resurrection of the Body.—The separation which takes place between the body and soul at death is not permanent. The body shall be raised from the dead on the last day and re-united to the soul from which it was parted. There shall be a "resurrection both of the just and the unjust" (Acts 24:15). "The time is coming when all that are in the graves shall hear His voice and shall come forth" (John 5:28). Believers and unbelievers shall indeed be raised for a different purpose, but they shall all be raised. In the case of the believers it will be a resurrection unto life; in that of the unbelievers, a resurrection unto damnation. The dead in Christ shall rise first.

The Body.—The resurrection will be the raising of the bodies that are in the graves, and not the creation of a new body. It will be essentially the same body which we had here on earth. But a great change will take place in it, even in the case of the unbelievers, and especially in that of the believers. Here the bodies of all men are mortal and corruptible. There they shall be immortal and incorruptible. This is true of the unbelievers also. For their body as well as their soul shall be punished eternally, and must therefore exist eternally.

But a far greater change shall take place in the believers. Their body shall not only be immortal and incorruptible, but shall be endowed with new and glorious properties. It shall be wholly freed from all the infirmities, imperfections and limitations to which it has been subject here on earth. It shall be a spiritual body like that of the Savior after His resurrection. For Christ shall change our vile body that it may be fashioned like unto His own glorious body. As we have borne the image of the earthy, we shall also bear the image of the heavenly. The body of the believer shall be made a fit tabernacle for the soul that shall inhabit for all eternity.

CHAPTER XXV. JESUS WILL COME AGAIN TO JUDGE THE LIVING AND THE DEAD.

The same Lord whom the apostles saw ascending into heaven from Mount Olivet shall come again in like manner as they saw Him go. He shall come in glory and majesty to judge the living and the dead. He will take the believers unto Himself, but will cast the unbelievers out from His presence forever.

When He Will Come.—The second coming of Jesus is certain. But the time of His coming no man knows. On that day and hour knows no man, not even the angels, but God only (Matt. 24:36). Even Christ Himself in His state of humiliation withheld from Himself the knowledge of that day. It shall come upon men unawares, like a thief in the night and like the flood in the days of Noah. "Like a snare it shall come upon all them that dwell on the face of the whole earth" (Luke 21:35). It shall find men eating and drinking, marrying and giving in marriage, with no thought of the coming of Christ and the final judgment. Because the Savior delays His coming, many scornfully ask, "Where is the promise of His coming; for since the fathers fell asleep all things continue as they were from the beginning of the creation?" (2 Pet. 3:4). But He delays His coming, in order that men may have opportunity to repent and be saved. What seems a long time to men is not long to God. "One day is with the Lord as a thousand years, and a thousand years as one day" (2 Pet. 3:8). When the proper time has arrived, Christ will come.

No One Can Compute the Time.—It is not possible to compute the date of Christ's second coming by means of arithmetical calculations from numbers mentioned in Old Testament prophecies or the book of Revelation, or from the chronology given in the margin of the Bible. That chronology is not inspired; it is not a part of the Bible. It is a careful but not infallible attempt to fix the date of Biblical events, and was placed in the Bible only a few hundred years ago as a matter of convenience to the reader. Books or pamphlets which profess to be able to calculate the date of the end of the world can only mislead, and are therefore to be shunned. The time of Christ's coming is meant to remain unknown to men; He will come when least expected, and not at the date on which men have calculated that He ought to come.

Signs of His Coming.—The second coming of Christ shall be preceded by signs. The Gospel shall first be preached throughout the entire world, and the Jews shall be converted to Christ. There shall be signs in the sun and in the moon and in the stars, deceivers and wicked men shall wax worse and worse, wars and tumults shall increase, the godly shall suffer intense persecution, and Antichrist, the man of sin and the human personification of wickedness and opposition to Christ, shall be revealed. Though these signs do not enable the believer to tell the day and the hour of Christ's coming, they serve to warn him of its nearness, and teach him to guard himself against worldly security so that he may be always ready.

How He Will Come.—The first time Jesus came to earth, He came in lowliness and humility; He came to suffer and die for men's sins. But when He comes again, it will be to judge the world. He shall come in the clouds with power and great glory, accompanied by all the holy angels.

How Regarded by Men.—The coming of Christ shall fill the wicked with terror and dismay. Those who during their lifetime lived in defiance of God, and spurned the offers of His grace, shall then cry out to the mountains and the rocks to fall on them and hide them from the face of Him that sits on the throne and from the wrath of the Lamb. For the day of His wrath shall have come, and they shall not be able to stand in His presence.

The believers on the other hand shall be filled with joy, because their redemption from all the evils of this world and their entrance on their eternal inheritance is at hand. For them Christ shall come in love and not in wrath. He shall come to receive them unto Himself forever.

The Judgment.—When Christ has come, all men shall be brought before His throne to judgment. For "we must all appear before the judgment seat of Christ; that every one may receive the things done in his body, according to that he hath done, whether it be good or bad" (2 Cor. 5:10). The dead shall be raised from their graves, or from the depths of the sea, or wherever their bodies may lie; and they, together with all who are alive at Christ's coming, shall be gathered before Him. Believers and unbelievers, great and small, from every nation and tribe, shall be summoned there to give an account of their life upon earth.

The Account.—Everything that men have done shall then be made manifest; every secret thing shall be revealed. Men shall be asked to give an account of all that they have done on the earth, even of every idle word that they have spoken. And the judgment shall be according to what men have done. Christ will render to every man according to his deeds, bestowing eternal life upon all who, by patient continuance in well-doing, have sought for glory, honor and immortality, but pouring out indignation and wrath, tribulation and anguish upon every soul that doeth evil. He shall reward every man according to his works.

Both believers and unbelievers shall be found to deserve eternal death by their sins. But the believers shall be justified by their faith in Christ. His righteousness shall cover up all their shortcomings, and shall be counted as if it belonged to them. They shall, therefore, escape the punishment which they have deserved by their sins; but the unbelieving, having nothing to plead, shall be sentenced to eternal death.

The Separation.—Christ shall separate the believers from the unbelievers, and place the believers upon His right hand and the unbelievers upon His left. Then shall He say to those on His right hand, "Come you blessed of my Father; inherit the kingdom prepared for you from the foundation of the world." And He shall say this to them, because they have shown by their works that they believe on Him. Then will He also say to those on His left hand, "Depart from me, you cursed, into everlasting fire prepared for the devil and his angels." He will condemn them, because they have shown by their deeds that they are impenitent and unbelieving. "These shall then go away into everlasting punishment: but the righteous into life eternal" (Matt. 25:31-36).

The End of the World.—With the coming of Christ to judgment, the present order of the world will come to an end. "The heavens shall pass away with a great noise, and the elements shall melt with fervent heat; the earth also and the works that are therein shall be burned up" (2 Pet. 5:10). For this reason the day of Christ's coming is called The Last Day. The earth itself has been contaminated by sin; it has been accursed for man's sake, and has become a home of disease and death. It is therefore reserved unto fire against the Day of Judgment, either to be annihilated or to be so completely purified and changed as to become a new earth. The whole creation is to be delivered from the bondage of corruption into the glorious liberty of the children of God. There shall be new heavens and a new earth, wherein dwells righteousness.

CHAPTER XXVI. THE ETERNAL DESTINY OF BELIEVERS AND UNBELIEVERS.

One of two destinies lies before every human being in the world to come. He will enter either upon eternal life in heaven or eternal death in hell. Which it shall be depends on the manner in which he conducts himself in this world toward the grace of God in Christ. The believers shall be saved; the unbelievers, lost.

Men Shape Their Own Destiny.—While it is true that all men are by nature dead in trespasses and sins and have no power of their own to save themselves, it is also true that God has provided salvation for all men, and through the Word of God gives them power to accept it. They may use this power and be saved by faith; or they may refuse to use it, and thus remain lost in their sins. In a very true sense, then, the shaping of his eternal destiny is in man's own hands. He will reap what he sows. "He that sows to his flesh shall of the flesh reap corruption; but he that sows to the Spirit shall of the Spirit reap life everlasting." When, on the day of judgment, the final and eternal destiny of men is decided by Christ, they shall be assigned to an eternity of joy or of woe according an their life in this world has shown the presence or absence of true and living faith.

Hell.—The impenitent and unbelieving shall spend their eternity in hell. They shall suffer eternal punishment in body and soul. Hell is not a mere fancy of man's brain, but a dreadful reality. It is attested by the plain words of Scripture. It is the place into which the wicked angels have been cast, and into which the impenitent and unbelieving among men shall be cast also. The rich man in the parable, who had not lived a life of faith, but had been lacking in love to God and his fellow-men and had left Lazarus lie unaided at his gate, awoke in hell and in torments and begged in vain for a single drop of water to cool his burning tongue.

The Torments of Hell.—The pain and misery of the lost is variously described in the Scriptures. They shall be cast into a furnace of fire. They shall be tormented by the worm that never dies and the fire that never is quenched (Mark 9:44). They shall be cast out into outer darkness, there shall be weeping and gnashing of teeth. Their own conscience shall perpetually reprimand them for their wickedness and folly in disobeying God and in refusing to accept the salvation which He so mercifully offered them. They shall be filled continually with remorse, despair and helpless rage. They shall be consumed by the fire of their own evil lusts, but be unable to gratify them. In absolute darkness and in total exclusion from God and from all that is good, they shall spend their eternity in ceaseless woe, in the company of the most wicked of men and of devils.

Degrees of Punishment.—The pains of hell will, indeed, differ in degree according to the measure of men's wickedness. The greater their iniquity and the greater the opportunities for salvation which they have despised, the deeper will be their remorse and anguish. But the sufferings of all the lost will be great beyond human power of expression, and beyond all the possible sufferings of this world. They shall be completely and forever forsaken by God, and excluded from every possibility of the enjoyment of any good. They shall be given over to the power and consequences of the sins from which they refused to be separated here.

Punishment Eternal.—The punishment of the lost will never end. The smoke of their torment shall ascend forever. God will not place them in hell for a season and then take them out of it. He will leave them there. Men must be fitted for heaven by the operation of God's grace in their hearts. If they have spurned that grace in this world, they will have to bear the, consequence of their folly in the next. Those who want to escape from the punishment of the next world must do so now. When they are once condemned to hell it will be too late. Between heaven and hell there is a gulf fixed, so that those who would pass from one side to the other cannot do so.

Heaven.—The believers shall have everlasting life, and shall dwell forever with the Lord in heaven. They shall inherit the kingdom prepared for them from the foundation of the world, and inhabit the heavenly mansions which Christ has gone to prepare for them. Their inheritance shall be one that is incorruptible, undefiled, and that fades not away.

Degrees of Glory.—All the believers shall enter upon an eternal inheritance in heaven. But the inheritance of all shall not be equally glorious. There shall be differences in glory, proportioned to the strength of their faith, the extent of their sufferings, and the zeal which they manifested in the service of Christ on earth. As one star differs from another star in glory, and the sun and the moon outshine them all, so there shall be differences in glory in those who are saved,—differences proportioned to the faithfulness which they have shown in those things with which Christ has entrusted them here. But while there will be differences of glory, all those who are saved shall be perfectly happy, just as the angels, though differing in rank, find perfect happiness in God's presence.

The Happiness of Heaven.—The bliss of heaven is so exalted, that we cannot form any adequate conception of it in this world. "Eye has not seen, nor ear heard, neither have entered into the heart of man the things which God has prepared for them that love Him" (1 Cor. 2:9). St. Paul saw some of the glories of heaven in a trance; but he could not and dared not describe them. We shall be able to comprehend and appreciate them only after we have entered upon their enjoyment.

Freedom from Every Evil.—While the happiness of heaven cannot be adequately described in the language of earth, the Bible nevertheless gives us some idea of the blessedness which there awaits the believers. They shall be freed from all annoyances, pains and sorrows. They shall neither hunger nor thirst; they shall not suffer from heat or cold. They shall have perfect rest and freedom from every ill of body and soul. The conflict against sin which continued throughout their life-time upon earth shall be over. They shall have won the victory and received the reward. There shall be no more sin in them, and they shall suffer no more consequences of sin. "God shall wipe away all tears from their eyes; and there shall be no more death, neither sorrow nor crying; neither shall there be any more pain, because the former things are passed away" (Rev. 21:4).

Dwelling in God's Presence.—The believers shall dwell forever in the light of God's presence, enjoy His love, and find in His service perfect and uninterrupted happiness. Freed from every vestige of sin, perfect in body and soul, they shall share in the glory of Christ, and live and reign with Him forever. All that was dark to them here on earth shall then become light. They shall see that all God's dealings with them in this world, however mysterious at the time, were prompted by His love and were needful in order to bring them to heaven at last. They shall regard all their earthly sufferings as unworthy to be compared with the glory that is then revealed in them. They shall learn more and more how great, how infinite is God's love. And in the company of the good angels and glorified men they shall never weary of serving Him and singing His glorious praise.

The Heavenly City.—In the twenty-first and twenty-second chapters of Revelation, St. John describes the glory of the heavenly city, the New Jerusalem, whose walls of jasper, set with precious stones, whose gates are of pearl, and whose streets are of gold. The city has no need of the sun or the moon to shine in it; for the glory of God lightens it and the Lamb is the light thereof. It is a city of endless day; for "there shall be no night there" (Rev. 18:25). "The throne of God and the Lamb shall be in it; and His servants shall serve Him: and they shall see His face" (Rev. 22:2-4).

www.ingramcontent.com/pod-product-compliance
Lightning Source LLC
Chambersburg PA
CBHW060807050426
42449CB00008B/1575

9780692216828